Nationalism

Fourth, expanded edition

Elie Kedourie

> We pieced our thoughts into philosophy,
> And planned to bring the world under a rule,
> Who are but weasels fighting in a hole.
> W. B. YEATS
> Nineteen Hundred and Nineteen

BLACKWELL Publishers

Copyright © Elie Kedourie, 1960, 1961, 1966
Editorial foreword © Sylvia Kedourie, 1993

The first edition, under the title *Nationalism* was published in 1960 by
Hutchinson & Co Ltd
Subsequent editions were published in 1961 and 1966 by Hutchinson
and the third edition was reprinted with revisions and Afterword in 1985.
This edition, with new Foreword and Introduction, first published in 1993
by Blackwell Publishers.

Reprinted 1994 (twice), 1996, 1998 (twice), 2000

Blackwell Publishers Ltd
108 Cowley Road
Oxford OX4 1JF, UK

Blackwell Publishers Inc.
350 Main Street
Malden, Massachusetts 02148, USA

British Library Cataloguing in Publication Data
A CIP catalogue record for this book is available from the British Library

Library of Congress Cataloging in Publication Data
Kedouri, Elie
Nationalism/Elie Kedourie – 4th, expanded edn.
p. cm.
Includes bibliographical references and index.
ISBN 0–631–18884–3 —— ISBN 0–631–18885–1 (paper)
1. Nationalism. I. Title
JC311.K37   1993
320.5'4—dc20

Typeset in 12 on 14 pt Sabon by Pentacor PLC, High Wycombe, Bucks
Transferred to digital print 2002

For Helen

CONTENTS

EDITORIAL FOREWORD

Elie Kedourie died suddenly and quite unexpectedly in Washington on 29 June 1992. He was, as ever, engaged on many projects. As a Fellow of the Woodrow Wilson International Center for Scholars, where he spent the last year of his life, he felt sufficiently released from all other commitments to devote most of his time to his book on Conservatism which had preoccupied him for many years. Unfortunately this will never be completed.

A glance at the conclusion to this book on nationalism, written over thirty years ago, will show that it is as valid today as it was when it was written. That his judgements and his exposition of historical events remain so sound after this passage of time only heightens the sense of loss, for his thoughts on contemporary and historical matters will no longer enlighten his readers. Amongst his papers, I found this essay which serves so well as the Introduction to a new edition of his *Nationalism*, a work of clear insight and classic precision.

Elie Kedourie was always perplexed by the subtle shades within which great numbers of peoples classified themselves or were classified by others. Labels identifying the 'national' affiliations of groups always worried him. His overriding concern was for the safety of the individual; he always saw clearly how this would be threatened by the imposition of ideological patterns. This worry of his is amply demonstrated by today's so-called 'ethnic cleansing'. The use of words with overtones of ritual purification makes the present phenomenon even more chilling.

Shifts in identification are even more acute when those in border areas change national identity as frontiers shift, and are drawn and redrawn. Europe has no lack of such frontiers where the resident population periodically finds itself under a different flag.

By including the following *Introduction*, I would like to draw the attention of the reader to the last four paragraphs which hint at the author's thoughts on such contemporary issues. They were numbered and were obviously written as reminders for further elaboration. Unfortunately Elie Kedourie had no time to develop these ideas on paper, but I decided to leave everything as I found it in his handwriting – save for deleting the numbers 1 to 4. In this I beg the reader's indulgence and understanding.

To end, I wish to acknowledge that it gives me pleasure, in the midst of grief, that a new edition of one of his books should keep his memory alive. I would like to thank Blackwell Publishers, and particularly Simon Prosser, for bringing out this commemorative edition.

Sylvia Kedourie
Spring 1993

INTRODUCTION TO THE
FOURTH EDITION

NATIONALISM has once again come to the fore. The collapse of the Soviet Union with the resulting conflicts between and within its former constituents has meant the disappearance of a political entity put together by the Tsars and inherited (and mismanaged) by the Bolsheviks. There is a sad irony in the collapse of Yugoslavia where a ferocious civil war opposes Serbians, Albanians, Croats and Bosnians. Yugoslavia was formed after the First World War as the concrete expression of the supposedly fervent desire of the South Slav nation (the Yugoslavs) to achieve the national unity for which they were preordained, but of which they had been deprived by conjugated rapacity and oppression at the hands of the Ottomans, Austrians and Hungarians.

These are by no means the only nationalist conflicts which have raged since the end of the Second World War. But because the collapse of the Soviet Union is the collapse of a super-power, and Yugoslavia is a European state, the conflicts which have arisen recently, that is within the last three or four years, have produced a particularly strong impression in the West. These conflicts have brought once more to the fore the issue of nationalism and its associated problems – in a sharp and acute form, and in a manner unknown in the last few decades. For me this is a striking development.

In 1960 I published *Nationalism*. It was really the text of a course of lectures which I gave at the London

School of Economics during the previous five years. I gave this course at the suggestion of the then Head of the Department of Government, Michael Oakeshott, who asked me to do so when I joined the department as an assistant lecturer in October 1953. I do not know what Oakeshott had in mind exactly when he made this request. For my own part, trained as I had been as an undergraduate in the history of ideas, it was as a problem in the history of ideas that I approached my assignment. The subject itself I had not much occasion to think about previously, and I was certainly not then concerned with nationalism as an urgent issue in current affairs – and I doubt if Michael Oakeshott himself saw it in this light. I think, rather, that for him this was one issue in the history of political thought which was weighty enough and difficult enough to merit putting before an audience of undergraduates in order to widen their intellectual horizons and stretch their minds. In this, I think, it was for him on a par with other organizing ideas in the political experience of the Western world – ideas such as the state of the sovereignty or representation or secularity which had their rise in the political experience of the West, but which have now spread to the rest of the world.

This at any rate was my own approach to the subject, as becomes evident on the most cursory examination of *Nationalism*. Of its six chapters four are concerned with tracing the intellectual origins of this ideology and examining its organizing ideas, their corollaries and implications. These organizing ideas, together with their implications are seen to be fully worked out by, at the latest, 1848 – a year which was described as the springtime of the nations, and which indeed saw, among much else, a great upsurge of nationalist claims and ambitions.

It is only the last two chapters which deal with the political history – as against the intellectual history – of nationalism. This political history involved a variety of ambitions and calculations by states (and social groups) which aspired to statehood in an international environment where an ideological style of politics came to be increasingly prevalent. The culmination of this state of affairs I saw happening during the First World War and its aftermath in which a large number of states appeared in central and eastern Europe and in the Middle East which professed to be based on the national principle. Just as important, the years after 1914 saw the explicit incorporation into international law of a moral idea – namely the right to national self-determination.

In 1953, when I started to think about the subject, as well as in 1960 when the book was published, I looked upon what I was doing as an attempt at historical explanation – and historical explanation is by definition concerned with the past. It is true that there were then active nationalist movements in the world, for instance the Algerian rebellion against French rule, but their existence did not pose new intellectual problems or invalidate the picture of nationalist politics as I presented it.

I have described nationalism as an ideology. In doing so, I mean to contrast it with constitutional politics. In constitutional politics the object in view is to attend to the common concerns of a particular society, to safeguard it against foreign assaults, to mediate disagreements and conflicts between various groups through political institutions, through legislation and the administration of justice, and to uphold the law as being above and beyond sectional interests however important or powerful.

Ideological politics is very different. Such a politics is concerned to establish a state of affairs in society and state such that everyone, as they say in old-fashioned novels, will live happily ever after. To do so, the ideologist will, to borrow Plato's analogy in the *Republic*, look upon state and society as a canvas which has to be wiped clean, so that his vision of justice, virtue and happiness can be painted on this *tabula rasa*.

Ideological politics in any real and substantial sense is a modern European phenomenon which appears at the time of the French Revolution. Kant's pamphlet of 1790 on *Perpetual Peace* may be said to express, and to argue for, such an ideological vision. Peace among men will reign only if all states are republics, and states are republics only if their citizens regulate their behaviour according to the categorical imperative. A moment's thought will show what an utter social and political upheaval will be required if such a state of affairs is to be established. A further moment's reflection will lead one to see that the very attempt to wipe the canvas clean must entail arbitrariness, lawlessness and violence on a stupendous scale, such that the ideological vision of perpetual peace and joy must recede further and further into the horizon. Ideological politics is thus necessarily and inevitably caught up in a perpetual disastrous and self- destructive tension between ends and means.

Curiously enough, the ideological current in Western political thought was itself a response to what some very powerful thinkers deeply felt to be the unhappy state of humanity in modern Europe. There was division between government and the governed. For the governed government was now an imposition from the outside, exerting an arbitrary force on its subjects – subjects seen by rulers as so many ciphers, mere abstract numbers in the statistical tables on which remote and faceless bureaucrats based their policies for the improvement and the welfare of their charges. However, such policies, devised in a spirit of impersonal and all-knowing benevolence, were in reality devoid of even the smallest spark of human sympathy or fellow-feeling.

A state operated on principles of this kind also meant division and separation between its individual members who could have no feeling of community and solidarity with one another. Treated as mere abstract numbers by their government, they themselves became accustomed to look upon their fellow-men in the same manner – (also as abstract ciphers with whom any relations were necessarily superficial, external and mechanical. Mirroring this division in society, echoing it so to speak, was a division in the soul of each man – division between head and heart, between reason and feeling. Reason was a mere computing, classificatory faculty quite unable to speak to feelings. This led to frustration, to self-stultification, and to a drying up of those imaginative powers – of that creativity which is man's glory distinguishing him from the rest of creation. Schiller's *Letters on the Aesthetic Education of Man*, published in the 1790s – a key document in the annals of alienation indeed in many thinkers, whose thought became very influential in succeeding decades in Europe – contributed to the sense of alienation which the conditions of modern life created.

The ideological currents in modern Western political thought were a response to the predicament of modern man identified in the manner I have described. The ideologies varied according to what was thought to be causing the alienation. In the event, two quite different ideologies became influential, powerful and prevalent in Europe, and later on in a wider world. One of these was nationalism which, briefly, saw humanity naturally divided into nations which were, which had to be, the proper unit of political organization. In the world, such as it was, political organization did not follow this principle, hence all the ills under which men suffered – oppression, alienation, and impoverishment of the spirit. Nothing would go well with humanity unless each nation enjoyed an independent existence in its own state. Furthermore if each nation lived and fulfilled itself in its own state, then, as Giuseppe Mazzini argued, there would come about perpetual peace in the world. This ideological obsession worked itself out in European and in world politics in the hundred years or so between 1848 and the end of the Second World War and its aftermath. It is, however, quite apparent now that this ideological obsession could provide no remedy for the ills of alienation and oppression for which it purported to provide a cure. Examples are numberless – Yugoslavia, Iraq, the issue of German unity, particularly between the wars – an issue which in fact served as the spark for a second world war. The greatest triumph of this ideological obsession is the enshrinement of national self-determination as the organizing principle of international order. Experience – bitter experience – has shown that contrary to the dreams of Mazzini and President Woodrow Wilson national self-determination is a principal of disorder, not of order, in international life. It is this which I tried to establish in the last two chapters of *Nationalism*.

The other powerful ideology which purported to provide a remedy for human alienation and unhappiness was socialism. The cause of these ills, as socialism diagnosed it, was private property. The first man who fenced in his property, as Rousseau argued, brought unfreedom into the world, and human beings will not taste freedom alike from oppression and self- alienation until private property is abolished. This other ideological obsession has in its turn been tested to destruction in twentieth-century politics. Like nationalism it has produced not happiness or spiritual fulfilment, or even material prosperity, but, on the contrary, unparalleled oppression and misery, and it has sunk by the weight of its own misconceived ideals.

The disintegration and failure of socialism in the Soviet empire and its satellites has not meant the disappearance of the ideological style of politics – far from it. As we can see it has produced, in a revulsion against socialist tyranny, a revival or recrudescence of nationalism – that other ideological obsession. Today, the argument of my book – an argument meant to be historical in character – has come to acquire an immediate relevance to current events – a relevance which was not intended or imagined when I was writing my lectures in the mid nineteen-fifties.

The implosion and self-destruction of Bolshevik and other Socialist regimes therefore does not mean that their succession will be affected peaceably or that the successor regimes will prove to be a success.

A nationalist aspiration does not signify *ipso facto* that the nations postulated by the ideology do in fact exist and can provide the social base for a nation-state, for example, Kazakh, Uzbek, Tajik and the Moldovan nations.

The problems which made a mockery of national self-determination after 1918 have once more reappeared: Uzbek-Armenian, Moldovan-Russian and many others.

The disappearance of the Soviet superpower, oppressive to its subjects as it was, has created a dangerous imbalance of power among its former components and between them and their neighbours. Possibility of serious conflicts exists. Russia, which by any definition is a Great Power in the classical sense, is bordered by the much weaker states which have broken away from the Soviet structure. As with water, power will find its level. Just as the security system set up at Versailles proved impotent to protect the successor states of Austria-Hungary from German power once Germany began to flex its muscles in the nineteen-thirties, so the UN system has no power to prevent Russia from dominating the former Tsarist and Soviet possessions. The impotence of the UN and of the EC in curbing Serbian ambitions in Croatia and Bosnia-Herzegovina may be a foretaste of what is yet to come elsewhere in Eastern Europe, the Caucasus and Central Asia. The perils resulting from Balkanization are not confined to the Balkans.

A nationalist ideology is clearly not *ipso facto* a guarantee of prosperity or of good and honest government. Thirty years of FLN rule in Algeria or the record of successive Iraqi, Syrian or Egyptian nationalist regimes, or of Yugoslavia under the monarchy as under Tito and his successors are a few examples which may serve as an illustration.

E. K.
Spring 1992

PREFACE TO THE SECOND EDITION

I HAVE taken the opportunity of a second edition to make a few changes and additions.

Noticing the first edition, some reviewers have remarked that I do not attempt to discuss whether nationalists should be conciliated or resisted. A decision on such an issue is necessarily governed by the particular circumstances of each individual case, and whether its consequences are fortunate or disastrous will depend on the courage, shrewdness and luck of those who have the power to take it. For an academic to offer his advice on this matter is, literally, impertinent: academics are not diviners, and it is only at dusk, as Hegel said, that the owl of Minerva spreads its wings.

E. K.
1961

PREFACE TO THE FIRST
EDITION

THIS book, it will be immediately obvious to the reader, would not have been possible but for the existence of a considerable body of European and American scholarship on which I could freely draw. The debt, extensive as it is, is not of the kind that can be repaid, except by making it ever greater. But I would like to mention in particular two great scholar whose works, though they do not deal with nationalism, have illuminated the subject for me; they are Albert Sorel and A. O. Lovejoy.

I would like to thank Mr. Ernest Gellner, Mr. Emile Marmorstein, and Professor Michael Oakeshott who took the trouble of discussing my argument with meticulous and friendly care, and of making many valuable suggestions. None of them, however, is responsible for what appears in the book.

E. K.
1960

1

POLITICS IN A NEW STYLE

NATIONALISM is a doctrine invented in Europe at the beginning of the nineteenth century. It pretends to supply a criterion for the determination of the unit of population proper to enjoy a government exclusively its own, for the legitimate exercise of power in the state, and for the right organization of a society of states. Briefly, the doctrine holds that humanity is naturally divided into nations, that nations are known by certain characteristics which can be ascertained, and that the only legitimate type of government is national self-government. Not the least triumph of this doctrine is that such propositions have become accepted and are thought to be self-evident, that the very word nation has been endowed by nationalism with a meaning and a resonance which until the end of the eighteenth century it was far from having. These ideas have become firmly naturalized in the political rhetoric of the West which has been taken over for the use of the whole world. But what now seems natural once was unfamiliar, needing argument, persuasion, evidences of many kinds; what seems simple and transparent is really obscure and contrived, the outcome of circumstances now forgotten and preoccupations now academic, the residue of metaphysical systems sometimes incompatible and even contradictory. To elucidate this doctrine it is necessary to enquire into the fortunes of certain ideas in the

philosophical tradition of Europe, and how they came
to prominence at this particular period.

The fortunes of ideas, like those of men, depend as
much on accident as on their own worth and character,
and if the doctrine of nationalism came into prominence
at the turn of the eighteenth century, this was the result
not only of a debate in which the philosophers were engaged, but also of events which invested the philosophical issues with immediate and obvious relevance.
The philosophy of the Enlightenment prevalent in
Europe in the eighteenth century held that the universe
was governed by a uniform, unvarying law of Nature.
With reason man could discover and comprehend this
law, and if society were ordered according to its
provisions, it would attain ease and happiness. The law
was universal, but this did not mean that there were no
differences between men; it meant rather that there was
something common to them all which was more
important than any differences. It might be said that all
men are born equal, that they have a right to life, liberty,
and the pursuit of happiness, or, alternatively, that men
are under two sovereign masters, Pain and Pleasure, and
that the best social arrangements are those which
maximize pleasure and minimize pain: whichever way
the doctrine is phrased, certain consequences can be
drawn from it. The state, on this philosophical view, is a
collection of individuals who live together the better to
secure their own welfare, and it is the duty of rulers so
to rule as to bring about – by means which can be
ascertained by reason – the greatest welfare for the
inhabitants of their territory. This is the social pact
which unites men together, and defines the rights and
duties of rulers and subjects. Such is not only the view
of the *philosophes*, for which they claimed universal
validity, but also the official doctrine of Enlightened
Absolutism.

According to this doctrine, the enlightened ruler regulates the economic activities of his subjects, provides them with education, looks after health and sanitation, supplies uniform and expeditious justice, and generally concerns himself – if need be even against their wishes – with his subjects' welfare, because the greatness of a state is the glory of its ruler, and a state can become great only in proportion to its population and to their prosperity. In this sense is to be understood the saying of Frederick the Great of Prussia, that a king is the first servant of the state. A small work cast in the form of letters between *Anapistemon* and *Philopatros*, written by Frederick himself, *Letters on the Love of the Fatherland* (1779), may illustrate these views. The author seeks to show that love of the fatherland is a rational sentiment and to rebut the idea, attributed to 'some encyclopaedist', that since the earth is the common habitation of our race, the wise man must be a citizen of the world. Of course, *Philopatros* concedes that men are brothers and should love one another; but this benevolence at large itself argues the existence of a duty more pressing and more specific, that towards the particular society with which the individual is linked by the social pact. 'The good of society', *Philopatros* informs *Anapistemon*, 'is yours. Without realizing it, you are so strongly tied to your fatherland, that you can neither isolate, nor separate yourself from it without feeling the consequence of your mistake. If the government is happy, you prosper; if it suffers harm, its misfortune will react on you. Similarly if the citizens enjoy an honest opulence, the Sovereign prospers, and if the citizens are overwhelmed with poverty, the condition of the Sovereign will be worthy of pity. Love of the fatherland is not therefore a mere concept of reason, it exists really.' And *Philopatros* goes on to point out that the integrity of all the state's provinces touches the citizen directly. 'Do you not see', he asks, 'that if the government were to lose these provinces, it would thereby become enfeebled, and losing consequently the resources it had drawn from them, would be less able than now to help you, in case of need?'

On this view, then, the cohesion of the state, and loyalty to it, depend on its capacity to ensure the welfare of the individual, and in him, love of the fatherland is a function of benefits received. Side by side with the King's argument, we may set that of a private person Goethe, reviewing in 1772 a book entitled *On the Love of the Fatherland,* written to promote loyalty to the Habsburgs in the Holy Roman Empire, had this to say: 'Have we a fatherland? If we can find a place where we can rest with our possessions, a field to sustain us, a home to cover us, have we not there a fatherland?'

Such was the current opinion in Europe at the outbreak of the French Revolution. It is essential to remember the significance of this event. It was not merely a civil disturbance, a *coup d'état,* which replaced one set of rulers by another. This was familiar to Europe, and the French Revolution was indeed widely taken at the outset to be one such commotion, or else an attempt to realize the programme of reforms which Enlightened Absolutism had officially made its own. But as became increasingly apparent the French Revolution introduced new possibilities in the use of political power, and transformed the ends for which rulers might legitimately work. The Revolution meant that if the citizens of a state no longer approved of the political arrangements of their society, they had the right and the power to replace them by others more satisfactory. As the Declaration of the Rights of Man and the Citizen had it: 'The principle of sovereignty resides essentially in the Nation; no body of men, no individual, can exercise authority that does not emanate expressly from it.' Here, then, is one prerequisite without which a doctrine such as nationalism is not conceivable. Such a doctrine would want to lay down how best a society should conduct its politics, and realize its aims, if need be by radical changes: the French Revolution showed, in a resounding manner, that such an enterprise was feasible. In this, it greatly strengthened a tendency for political restlessness implicit in the reforms preached by the Enlightenment and ostensibly adopted by Enlightened Absolutism. These reforms were to be made according to a plan; and they were not to cease until society in all its particulars conformed to this plan. There grew, thus, an eager expectation of change, a prejudice in its favour, and a belief that the state stagnated unless it was constantly innovating. Such a climate of thought was necessary for the development and spread of doctrines like nationalism.

'The principle of all sovereignty resides essentially in the Nation.' What, then, was meant by a nation? *Natio* in ordinary speech originally meant a group of men belonging together by similarity of birth, larger than a family, but smaller than a clan or a people. Thus, one spoke of the *Populus Romanus* and not of the *natio romanorum*. The term applied particularly to a community of foreigners. Medieval universities were, it is well known, divided into 'nations': the University of Paris had four nations: *l'honorable nation de France, la fidèle nation de Picardie, la vénérable nation de Normandie*, and *la constante nation de Germanie*; these distinctions in use within the university, indicated places of provenance, but in no way corresponded either to modern geographical divisions, or indeed to what is now understood by 'nations'. Thus the *nation de France* referred to speakers of Romance languages including Italians and Spaniards; the *nation de Picardie* referred to the Dutch, that of Normandie to those originating from North-Eastern Europe, and that of *Germanie* to Englishmen as well as to Germans proper. By extension, the word came to be used as a collective noun, sometimes in a pejorative sense. Thus Machiavelli speaks of the ghibelline nation, and Montesquieu refers to monks as the pietistic nation. This use of the word as a collective noun persists into the eighteenth century, and we find Hume stating in his essay *Of National Characters* that 'a nation is nothing but a collection of individuals' who, by constant intercourse, came to acquire some traits in common, and Diderot and D'Alembert in the Encyclopédie defining 'nation' as 'a collective word used to denote a considerable quantity of those people who inhabit a certain extent of country defined within certain limits, and obeying the same government'. But the word also developed in time a special political meaning. A nation came to be understood as that body of persons who could claim to represent, or to elect representatives for, a particular territory at councils, diets, or estates. Church Councils were divided into nations; the Estates General of France meeting in 1484 comprised six nations; at the Peace of Szatmar of 1711, which ended the fighting between the Imperial forces and the Hungarians, the parties to the settlement were the Habsburg dynasty and the Hungarian nation: in such a context 'nation' did not mean the generality of the people inhabiting the territory of Hungary, but the 'barons, prelates, and nobles of Hungary', an exceedingly small part of the population, who nevertheless constituted to use Guizot's fruitful distinction, at once the *pays légal* and the pays *réel*. Such is the sense in which Montesquieu uses the term in *The Spirit of the Laws*, when he says that 'under the first two dynasties [in France] the nation was often called together, that is the lords and the bishops'. Therefore, when the revolutionaries stated that 'the principle of sovereignty resides essentially in the Nation' they may be taken to have asserted that the Nation was more than the King and the Aristocracy. This is the claim implicit in Diderot's and D'Alembert's definition just quoted, and later made quite explicit by Sieyès. 'What is a nation?' asked Sieyès. 'A body of associates living under one common law and represented by the same legislature.'

Such a claim is both simple and comprehensive. A nation is a body of people to whom a government is responsible through their legislature; any body of people associating together, and deciding on a scheme for their own government, form a nation, and if, on this definition, all the people of the world decided on a common government, they would form one nation. But such an inference, though correct, is merely academic. Another inference could, however, be drawn, the effects of which were not as negligible. Suppose a number of individuals, living under a certain government, decide that they no longer wish to continue under it; since the sovereignty is theirs, they may now form a new government and constitute a nation on their own. Such a principle introduced into eighteenth-century Europe was bound to create turmoil. Relations between its states were the outcome of accidents, wars, or dynastic arrangements, and were regulated by the play of conflicts and alliances, of friendships and antagonisms which somehow managed to produce a balance of power. It may be that such a balance had no intrinsic merits of its own, that it was neither a principle of order nor a guarantee of rights, but a mere empirical contrivance liable to frequent and serious breakdown. But the working of such a balance rested on an assumption which itself served to limit and control any breakdown. This assumption was that the title of any government to rule did not depend on the origin of its power. Thus the society of European states admitted all varieties of republics, of hereditary and elective monarchies, of constitutional and despotic régimes. But on the principle advocated by the revolutionaries, the title of all governments then existing was put in question; since they did not derive their sovereignty from the nation, they were usurpers with whom no agreement need be binding, and to whom subjects owed no allegiance. It is clear that such a doctrine would envenom international quarrels, and render them quite recalcitrant to the methods of traditional statecraft; it would indeed subvert all international relations as hitherto known.

Soon enough an issue arose which exhibited to the world the consequences of this new doctrine. When Alsace was joined to the French kingdom in the seventeenth century, the position of the nobility in the province was regulated by international treaty. Those among them who owned estates both in Alsace and in the Holy Roman Empire owed allegiance to the King of France in respect of their Alsatian estates, and, on the other hand, in respect of their Imperial territories, enjoyed the status to which they were entitled under the constitution of the Empire. Shortly after the outbreak of the Revolution all feudal privileges were abolished in France, and the rights of the Alsace nobility came into question. They owed, it is true, allegiance to the King and were therefore, to this extent, bound by French laws, but this allegiance, on the other hand, had been created by an international treaty and their privileges, it was argued, were guaranteed by the same treaty. These privileges, it was represented, could not be touched unless the revolutionary government was prepared to commit a breach of the treaty. The revolutionaries recognized that special considerations applied and offered, as an act of grace, to compensate the Alsace nobility for the privileges they had abolished. But this unilateral action did not satisfy the Alsatian nobles: if their privileges were to be tampered with, let the French government negotiate, in the proper way, a new settlement, instead of handing down arbitrary decrees. The debate went on; and what was said on the French side is worthy of notice. The Constituent Assembly had referred the question to a special committee, and its *rapporteur* began his report by defining the new principle on which France would henceforth conduct her foreign policy. The incorruptible representatives of the French people, he said, having proclaimed the sacred and inalienable rights of the nations, recognize no other rule but that of Justice. Therefore all previous treaties and conventions which are the fruit of the error in which kings and their ministers were lost will no longer have force. The old international law was one thing, and the new one quite another. According to the old principles, the nobles of Alsace could rightly claim compensation under the treaty, but in the new era all is changed. The French nation had declared itself sovereign, and the people of Alsace, by an act of their will, united themselves to the French people and shared in their sovereignty. The union of France and Alsace is now legitimate not by virtue of any treaty, but by virtue of the manifest will of the people. The nobles have no right to compensation, since the will of the people has not stipulated that they should be offered any. 'Has the free union of one people with another', asked Robespierre in a debate, 'anything in common with conquest?' Similarly, what would have been confiscation before 1789 was, afterwards, a mere entering into lawful possession. Such were the miracles possible under the new dispensation.

The revolutionaries, then, were claiming the pacific exercise of an obvious natural right, and in the process, offering to the world a new international law which, they stated, would necessarily lead to peace. Article VI of the Constitution of 1790 declared: 'The French nation renounces all wars of conquest, and will never employ her forces against the freedom of any people.' But the principle apparently admitted of an elastic interpretation, for it could still be used to justify the use of armies outside France. Barely two years after these categorical declarations, a decree of the Convention declared that the French nation, while it would not embark on a war against another nation, deemed it right to defend a free people against the unjust aggression of a king, and a later decree directed the executive power to give help to peoples struggling in the cause of liberty. The new international law, then, could not abolish quarrels and wars. France was still France, a state among European states with ambitions and views, and possessing the power to enforce them on other weaker states. What the new principles did was to introduce a new style of politics in which the expression of will overrode treaties and compacts, dissolved allegiance, and, by mere declaration, made lawful any act whatever. By its very nature, this new style ran to extremes. It represented politics as a fight for principles, not the endless composition of claims in conflict. But since principles do not abolish interests, a pernicious confusion resulted. The ambitions of a state or the designs of a faction took on the purity of principle, compromise was treason, and a tone of exasperated intransigence became common between rivals and opponents. Consciousness of right bred a righteousness which excesses could never destroy, but only confirm. Terrorism became the hallmark of purity: 'There is nothing', exclaimed St Just, 'which so much resembles virtue as a great crime.' It seemed, indeed, as though great crimes were the only way to ensure justice: 'There is something terrible', St Just also said, 'in the sacred love of the fatherland; it is so exclusive as to sacrifice everything to the public interest, without pity, without fear, without respect for humanity. . . . What produces the general good is always terrible.' This style, spread and established by a successful revolution, found increasing favour in Europe after 1789. Under its influence doctrines like nationalism were developed and perfected. But it was not the French Revolution only which tended to such a result. Another revolution, in the realm of ideas, worked powerfully to second its action.

2

SELF-DETERMINATION

THE philosophy which found expression in the revolutionary pronouncements did not constitute a homogeneous system. Men, the revolutionaries asserted, possessed inalienable natural rights; society ought to be so arranged as to foster these rights; and the *ancien régime* was evil precisely because it violated them. To speak of natural rights, however, assumes the existence of an orderly universe, capable of rational explanation, of natural laws holding sway over both men and things, and the difficulty was that the fashionable philosophy of the enlightenment made such an assumption extremely difficult. This philosophy rejected alike Plato, Aristotle, and the Biblical account of the Creation, those systems which had hitherto supplied in Europe a principle of order, to justify and make bearable the disorder and incoherence of the world. And at the very time when political orators were proclaiming the coming reign of justice and right, the labours of the philosophers were tending to show that these things were obscure, uncertain, and incapable of rational proof. The theory of knowledge which found most favour in the Enlightenment held that only our senses made possible our acquaintance with the external world. The mind is, in the beginning, a clean slate, on which, gradually, sensations leave their mark. Sensations and the memory of sensations constitute the basis of our knowledge; they enable us to compare and contrast, to foresee and take thought; on them alone ultimately are based man's most abstruse philosophies and his most intricate artifacts. But if such is the case, then we are the prisoners of our sensations, and cannot escape from them. Sensations lack substance, they deceive, they are various and changeable; they cannot provide insight into the structure of the universe, for natural laws cannot be felt, and orderliness cannot be touched. What sensations can provide, at most, are probabilities or expectations, the skill of the water-diviner, not the sure path of the scientist. Further, if such is the nature of knowledge, how are we to assert that liberty, equality, and fraternity are the birthright of every individual, how at all indeed to lay down any rule of behaviour which can withstand critical scrutiny; which does not, at length, dissolve into a perplexing haze of opinion and sensations? Liberty and all the rest may well exist and have reality, but the question was how to prove it, and on this philosophy proof seemed impossible.

It was the achievement of the philosopher Immanuel Kant (1724–1804) to show a way out of the predicament, a way which seemed, and not only in the eyes of fellow–philosophers, satisfactory and convincing. His solution provided a new certainty to replace the old metaphysical certainties which had ceased to attract. His claim, it is true, was more modest; the certainty he aimed at could rest neither on revelation nor on high metaphysical grounds; only on what the mind, proceeding critically on its own, could achieve. But modest and critical as it looked, Kant's philosophy soared higher than any metaphysic and issued in claims as sweeping as any dogma. In ethics, Kant proceeded to a Solomon's judgement. It was useless to seek to prove matters of morality by methods used for the understanding of nature. From the nature of things, we cannot deduce the worth we ought to put on them. The root of all the perplexity which had hitherto obtained lay in this, that philosophers were attempting to prove laws of morality as though they were laws of physics. Such an attempt led either to an indefensible dogmatism, or, by an obvious reaction, to utter scepticism. Morality and liberty existed, everybody knew that, felt it rather in their bones, and acted accordingly; difficulties began to arise the moment it was attempted to put this certainty in scientific dress. Knowledge was of the phenomenal world, a world, some held, of inexplicable contingencies, and others, of iron necessities, and if morality were derived from this kind of knowledge then we could never be free but always the slave either of contingency or of blind impersonal laws. Morality had therefore to be separated from knowledge. Morality is the outcome of obedience to a universal law which is to be found within ourselves, not in the world of appearances. For morality to be possible, it must be independent of the laws which govern appearances. 'Such independence', writes Kant in the *Critique of Practical Reason* (1788), 'is called *freedom* in the strictest, i.e. transcendental sense.'

This definition of freedom has far-reaching implications which may be appreciated when compared with those of another, and seemingly simpler, view. 'Freedom', we read in the *Institutes of Justinian*, 'is a man's natural capacity of doing what he pleases unless he is prevented by force or law.' But such a view, pushed to its logical conclusion, becomes hardly tenable; for no man, according to this notion, could be entirely free, unless he were alone in the world, or the master of all other men, since otherwise the possibility would always be present of someone standing in his path and impeding his freedom. But this is not all, because even if such a man existed, he would still not be free; he would still be subject to the demands of his body, and would have to eat, drink, and sleep. Freedom in this view is, then, so hemmed in and circumscribed that it is doubtful whether it can still be called freedom. The alternative, Kantian, view escapes these difficulties. Man, it holds, is free when he obeys the laws of morality which he finds within himself, and not in the external world. Only when the will of man is moved by such an inward law can it really be free, and only then can there be talk of good and evil, of morality and justice. If virtue exists, it does not reside in an object, it does not consist in obedience to some external authority, or in the feeling of well-being which accompanies certain actions; virtue is the quality of the free will when it obeys the inward law. 'Nothing', Kant begins the *Groundwork of the Metaphysic of Morals* (1785), 'can possibly be conceived in the world, or even out of it, which can be called good without qualification, except a Good Will.' Morality is independent of consequences, and impervious to rewards. A man can be imprisoned in the worst of dungeons, or suffer the most odious of tyrannies, but he may still be free, if his will is free; and his will is free when it is acting in accordance with the categorical imperative, as Kant denotes this inward law. All this may be considered a brilliant account – not, however, without its difficulties – of the moral life, an account which has affinities with Stoicism, with the Judeo-Christian tradition, and particularly with Lutheranism. Kant was as much against sin as the strictest moralist of any other persuasion; he also wanted to affirm the existence of God, freedom, and morality. He differed from his predecessors only in the manner in which he sought to prove these things. Indeed, he himself, in the preface to the *Critique of Practical Reason*, denied that he was proposing a new principle of morality; what he was offering, he said, was 'only a new formula'.

What was this formula? Its originality consisted in the manner in which the categorical imperative was presented. It was totally independent of nature and of external command. So for Luther the salvation of the Christian depended not on works, but on faith, that is, on a state of inward grace, and Christian liberty was the result of full submission to the Word of God. But Luther was quite clear that the faith which was efficacious for salvation was a specific faith in a divine Revelation, in the commands of God, in the Crucifixion, and in its supernatural redemptive effects; these it would have never occurred to him to question. 'Our works', said the Augsburg Confession of 1530, 'cannot reconcile us to God or merit remission of sins and grace and justification. This we obtain only by faith. . . .' 'Men are warned', the Confession added, 'that the word faith does not signify merely the knowledge of an event (the devils and impious men have that), but it signifies a faith which believes not in an event merely, but also in the effect of an event.' For Kant, however, the categorical imperative, obedience to which makes free, is not a divine command. It is a command which wells up within the soul, freely recognized and freely accepted. Just as the natural world cannot be the source of moral value, so neither can the will of God. If the will of God is the ground of the categorical imperative, then man's actions are dictated by an external command, freedom disappears, and morality becomes meaningless. This then is Kant's 'new formula', that the good will, which is the free will, is also the autonomous will. For it to be good, it has to choose good freely, and what that good shall be, the will itself legislates for itself. As if to emphasize the imperial nature of this legislative will, Kant expressly declares that in so doing it is as though saying: *Sic volo, sic iubeo,* This is my will and my pleasure.

For all its professions of modesty, such a doctrine is sweeping in what it claims, and annihilatory in what it rejects, and there is point in the poet Heine's remark, that, as a revolutionary, Kant puts Robespierre quite in the shade. For Kant's doctrine makes the individual, in a way never envisaged by the French revolutionaries or their intellectual precursors, the very centre, the arbiter, the sovereign of the universe. In the eyes of this doctrine, he is not a mere element in the natural order and possessed, as such, of the right to liberty and equality; it is rather the individual who, with the help of self-discovered, self-imposed norms, determines himself as a free and moral-being. Nowhere is the radical character of such a claim made clearer than in the curious argument which Kant uses in the *Critique of Practical Reason* to establish the existence of God. Dogmas which purport to prove this by metaphysical arguments will not survive critical scrutiny; they themselves rather are the enemy of religion, for, as they are inevitably proved erroneous, men will turn atheist; and yet there is need to believe in the existence of God. How then to satisfy this need? The categorical imperative, Kant reasons, imposes on us the duty to promote the highest good; but to further the highest good assumes that it can exist; and if it is necessary to assume the highest good, then it is necessary to assume the existence of God, a perfect being, since an imperfect being could not be the source of the highest good: 'This presupposition [the highest good] is made only under the condition of the existence of God, and this condition inseparably connects this supposition with duty. Therefore', he concludes, 'it is morally necessary to assume the existence of God.' The existence of God then depends on the need of man; God is an assumption which man makes in asserting his moral freedom. The inversion of the traditional order of thought, in which man was the creature of God, is complete. Here, in order to defend religion, Kant sees no other alternative but to make God the creature of man.

The logic of this doctrine was carried further. The end of man was to determine himself as a free being, self-ruling and self-moved, and religion, rightly understood, was the perpetual quest for perfection. What counted was the activity itself, not its particular manifestations at one time or another, in one place or another. The quest was endless, and to confuse it with dogmas and beliefs, themselves the result of past searchings, was to impede the free activity of man in search of his perfection. So the Lutheran theologian Friedrich Schleiermacher (1768-1834), developing the mode of thought inaugurated by Kant, refused to allow belief in God to interfere with true religion. 'Religion', wrote Schleiermacher in his *Addresses on Religion* (1789), 'is the outcome neither of the fear of death, nor of the fear of God. It answers a deep need in man. It is neither a metaphysic, nor a morality, but above all and essentially an intuition and a feeling. . . . Dogmas are not, properly speaking, part of religion: rather it is that they are derived from it. Religion is the miracle of direct relationship with the infinite; and dogmas are the reflection of this miracle. Similarly belief in God, and in personal immortality, are not necessarily a part of religion; one can conceive of a religion without God, and it would be pure contemplation of the universe; the desire for personal immortality seems rather to show a lack of religion, since religion assumes a desire to lose oneself in the infinite, rather than to preserve one's own finite self.' Religion for Schleiermacher is only the spontaneous expression of a free will. For such a doctrine, everything, in the end, must contribute to the self-determining activity of the autonomous individual and the universe itself is only there to minister to his self-cultivation. 'Every good man', asserted Friedrich Schlegel (1772-1829), Schleiermacher's friend, 'ceaselessly becomes more and more God. To become God, to be Man, to cultivate oneself, are expressions which all have the same meaning.'

Theology exhibits well the tendencies of Kantian doctrine, but its influences of course extended in other directions. Intimate conviction, needing support from nothing external, came to be seen as the true guide to political action. After the Napoleonic wars, a society of radical students, the *Burschenschaft*, was set up in the university of Jena to work for unity and democracy in Germany. One of its leaders preached that the righteous man recognizes no external law; once convinced that a course of action was right, he had unconditionally and uncompromisingly to realize the dictates of reason as revealed to him. Among the adepts this was known simply as 'the principle', and those who followed it hence termed themselves the 'Unconditionals'; they took Jesus as their hero, for they considered him a martyr to conviction, and their association-song proclaimed: 'A Christ thou shalt become.' One of these students, Carl Sand, acquired the conviction that the writer, Kotzebue, was an enemy of the German people, and decided to kill him. Having done the deed, he left a paper by the side of his victim on which was inscribed: 'A Christ thou shalt become.' The inscription, of course, referred to Sand, not to his victim.

This is not to say that Kant himself would have acquiesced in such uses to which his doctrine was put. When he himself wrote specifically on political questions, he was an amalgam of audacity and timorousness, preaching at the same time strict obedience to the state, and hinting also at views which could lead to the subversion of all settled authority. When a philosopher launches a system upon the world, he cannot be held responsible for the implications which others may rightly draw from it. Implications are not a matter of logic alone, they depend on judgement, experience, and circumstances. Implications which the inventor of a system may consider fantastic, far-fetched, or negligible may not seem so to his continuators. Even then, Kant's statements on politics do show what significance autonomy of the will, considered as a political doctrine, can possess. In his treatise on *Perpetual Peace* (1794), Kant set out the conditions he considered necessary to a stable, peaceful international order. The First Definitive Article for Perpetual Peace by which states would have to bind themselves, Kant thought, would be that the civil constitution of every state should be republican. A republican state, for Kant, was one where, regardless of the forms of government, the laws were or could be the expression of the autonomous will of the citizens. Only in such a situation could peace be guaranteed. It is, of course, extremely improbable for such a prospect to be realized, but even seriously to look upon it as an ideal to which relations between states ought as much as possible to approximate would seem to introduce a new factor of turmoil in international relations. Kant himself argued in *The Metaphysic of Morals* (1797) that the 'origin of power is practically *inscrutable* to the people who are placed under its authority', and that 'the subject ought not actively to probe too deeply into its origin as if the obedience which he owes to the supreme power was a debatable right'. But this other principle, that states ought to be republican in constitution, meant that the origins of any state whatever and the title of its rulers were under the perpetual scrutiny of seditious subjects and ambitious neighbours, that settlements could be retracted and compacts dishonoured on the pretext that a republican constitution was lacking, or that the very breaking of a contract would itself advance the prospect of such a constitution. In this, of course, Kant merely reinforced the teaching which the French Revolution spread with such success over Europe and the world. It may be argued, however, that Kant was not an agitator, that he was speaking *ad clerum*, addressing fellow-philosophers, who knew how to understand his words, and who were familiar with the difference between the teachings of philosophy and the necessities of power. Again, it may be argued that Kant ought to be read as a moralist, not as a writer on politics, that his genius served to exhibit the inescapable conditions of moral behaviour. But Kant did attempt, as has been seen, to discuss politics in terms of his ethical doctrine, and, further, his words were written down in books for all to read, and of those who read and were convinced, there happened then to be many who believed that philosophy held the key to right political behaviour. It was they indeed who enlarged so greatly the scope of Kant's doctrine of the autonomy of the will, and drew from it far-reaching political conclusions.

Other political aspects of this doctrine appear in Kant's writings. Kant was greatly excited by the French Revolution, defended it, and acclaimed it as a milestone in human history. Though he looked with horror on the execution of Louis XVI, in his *Religion Within the Limits of Pure Reason* (1793) he explained in this way the excesses of the Revolution: 'One must be free in order to learn how to use one's powers freely and usefully. To be sure, the first attempts will be brutal, and will bring about a more painful and more dangerous state than when one was under the orders, but also under the protection of a third party. However, one never ripens into reason except through one's own experiences, and one must be free in order to be able to undergo them.' Here is evident with particular clarity that process of reasoning which makes autonomy the essential end of politics. A good man is an autonomous man, and for him to realize his autonomy, he must be free. Self-determination thus becomes the supreme political good. For its sake Kant is prepared to accept brutality; to it he subordinates all the other benefits of social life; self-government, as a well-known slogan was later to put it, is better than good government. 'For', he says in *The Dispute of the Faculties* (1798), the last treatise he published, 'the being endowed with freedom is not content to enjoy a pleasant life, which might fall to his lot through the action of another . . . what matters is the principle by means of which he procures it.'

Kant's ethical teachings, then, expressed and propagated a new attitude to political and social questions; they made popular among the intellectual classes of Germany a new political temper. Moral strenuousness became the hallmark of virtue; a course of action could not be good unless it were the outcome of deep moral struggle. 'Virtue', wrote Kant in *The Metaphysic of Morals*, 'is the strength of a man's maxims in following his duty. All strength is known by the hindrances which it can overcome; with virtue, these are the natural inclinations, which can come in conflict with the moral prescription; and since it is man himself who puts these hindrances in the way of his maxims, virtue is not only compulsion of oneself . . . but a compulsion according to a principle of inner freedom.' Struggle, then, must accompany all attempts to realize virtue, in society as well as in oneself. Struggle is the guarantee of higher intentions, and compromise a surrender to base instincts. The autonomous man is a stern activist, a perpetually tormented soul. A politics fashioned in his image is a politics where struggle *per se* is a necessary feature.

Another facet of this temper is its tendency to divorce morality from nature and history. Morality proceeds from self-legislation, and may not be shackled by things as they are. The only legitimate limits are self-imposed limits. Others are as nothing to the autonomous man. 'The only impossibility of which I am aware', wrote Schleiermacher in his *Soliloquies* (1800), 'is to transcend the limits which I freely placed upon my nature from the beginning; the only things I cannot do are those which I surrendered in deciding what I wanted to become; naught else is impossible for me save to reverse the original decision as once taken. . . . My only purpose is ever to become more fully what I am; each of my acts is but a special phase in the unfolding of this single will. . . Come then what may! My will rules fate, as long as I relate everything to this comprehensive purpose, and remain indifferent to external conditions. . . .' The free man asserts himself against the world; by the strength of his soul he bends it to his will, for conviction can move mountains; and his head is bloody but unbowed. This characteristic euphory is the product of self-determination. As important as the substance of the doctrine are these habits and attitudes which it encouraged and fostered. They helped to make self-determination a dynamic doctrine. Nationalism, which is itself, as will be seen, largely a doctrine of national self-determination, found here the great source of its vitality, and it has therefore been necessary to examine how self-determination came to have this central importance in ethical and political teachings.

3

STATE AND INDIVIDUAL

THE idea of self-determination as the highest moral and political good inevitably produced a deep change in the tone of political speculation. A society of autonomous men could not be that collection of individuals possessed of inalienable natural rights which, to the French revolutionaries, constituted the sovereign nation. Autonomy is not a condition achieved here and now, once and for all; it is rather to be struggled for ceaselessly, perhaps never to be attained or permanently secured. What shall we conceive the role of the state to be in a world perpetually struggling for perfection? It was not so much Kant himself, as those who claimed to be his disciples and continuators, who provided a rounded and systematic doctrine of the state based on the new ideas. But here again, the influence of Kant's thought was decisive; the solutions he provided for the problems of philosophy, and the difficulties which these solutions raised in turn, left a lasting, unmistakable imprint on subsequent speculation.

Kant's object in his critical philosophy was to provide a sure, incontrovertible account of the scope and limits of human knowledge, without making, on the one hand, metaphysical assertions incapable of proof, or, on the other, falling into the radical scepticism to which a theory of knowledge exclusively based on sensation seemed to lead. It is to this end that he separated morality from scientific knowledge, and to this end that he offered in the *Critique of Pure Reason* (1st edition, 1781) an account of how a scientific knowledge of the world was at all possible. Kant's theory was that knowledge of the world was an outcome of two co-operating factors: sensations impinge on a perceiving self which, with the help of categories inherent in it, imposes a synthetic intelligible unity on what would, otherwise, remain a chaos of unrelated and incoherent impressions. These categories are not abstracted from perception; they are logically prior to and independent of any experience; they constitute the form in which scientific knowledge must present itself to and be known by our human minds. These categories, Kant believed, could be discovered by studying the presuppositions of arithmetic, Euclidean geometry, Newtonian physics, and traditional logic. But the sensations which the categories of our mind transform into objective experience we only know in space and time. Now space and time, Kant argued, are not properties of things; they are rather something contributed by the perceiving self to the sensations impinging on it. They are forms of perception into which all things are inevitably moulded before we can ever take cognizance of them, compulsory spectacles which we have to put on before we can see anything whatever. The conclusion which follows from such a view is that we can never know things as they really are, as they exist in themselves independent of our observation. To know the world is to change it into what it is not. The error can never be corrected; Achilles can never overtake the tortoise.

Such a conclusion abounds in difficulties and must cause the philosophic mind acute discomfort. Consider the situation: the perceiving self receives sensations from the outside, and these sensations can only emanate from things-in-themselves; but precisely because they do send out these sensations, which come to the perceiving self in space and time, things-in-themselves can never be known. Again, perception in the perceiving self must be caused by things-in-themselves, but causation takes place in space and time, and things-in-themselves are outside time and space; how then can they have effects in space and time? Further, if things-in-themselves are to remain for ever outside the circle of human understanding, is Kantian epistemology an improvement on that which derives all knowledge from the mere passive reception of sensations? On neither theory is certainty possible, on neither can the mind know the world as it really is. In one case the mind is the slave of its sensations, and in the other of its categories; in both it is wedded to appearance, and may not know reality. Reality gives rise to appearance, yet it is always hidden behind a cloud, and no man may see it.

Things-in-themselves were crucial to Kant's argument, and yet, in a philosophy which claimed to be critical, they once again introduced metaphysics, and remained a disturbing element, rebellious to proof, lacking all evidence, and giving rise to intractable difficulties. It is clear that Kant's system could not stay as it was; but one thing at least was established: that an epistemology exclusively based on sensation was unsatisfactory since it led ultimately to radical scepticism and destroyed all possibility of certain knowledge. Philosophical progress lay then in removing from Kant's system the difficulties which beset it, and in making it fully critical, completely systematic, and wholly rational. Quite a few of Kant's disciples attempted the emendation of his doctrines, and of these one of the earliest and most influential was Johann Gottlieb Fichte (1762-1814). Fichte considered that his own doctrine did away with the difficulties of the Kantian system and indeed claimed that what he taught was but 'the

Kantian doctrine properly understood' and 'genuine criticism consistently carried out'. Kant needed things-in-themselves in order to distinguish between reality and fantasy, to emphasize the independence of the world from the perceiving self, and to account for the general agreement which obtains among men regarding its features. But if things-in-themselves guaranteed that this world was not a dream, they also, as has been seen, raised difficulties as awkward as those which they were claimed to solve. Was it not self-defeating to appeal to things-in-themselves? Fichte argued that for us to assert the existence and reality of anything was to assert that it existed, that it was real for us, in our own consciousness; and beyond or behind our own consciousness it was impossible for us to go. It was self-contradiction to say that things-in-themselves existed, but that, nonetheless, we could not know them; either we knew them, or else they did not exist. Kant's account of the possibility and the limits of human knowledge was therefore quite inadequate. It was not merely that categories which inhered in the mind imposed unity and coherence on a flow of sensations which emanated from a source independent of the mind. Rather it was that both categories and sensations, indeed the world as we know it, are all the product of the consciousness, manufactured, so to speak, by it: if his doctrine, Fichte wrote, 'should be asked how things-in-themselves are constituted, the answer must be: As we have to make them.' But then, if the world is made by the consciousness, who is to say that it is not a fabrication of fancy, and that such a theory of knowledge is a confession of defeat, a retreat into fantasy? Again, if the world is made by the consciousness, how can the theory account for the fixity and determinateness of external experience which in Kant's doctrine was ascribed to the existence of things-in-themselves? Fichte here argued that, just as an individual consciousness makes its own world, and nothing outside this consciousness can form part of this particular world, so the world as a whole, nature in all its variety and history in its past, present, and future, must necessarily be the product of a universal consciousness, an Ego which embraces everything within itself, and of which everything that happens is a manifestation. This Ego transcends all individuals, and constitutes for them the guarantee for the stability of the world, its orderliness and rationality; and by means of their reason, men can discriminate between mere fantasy and the product of the universal consciousness. Such a theory, Fichte held, avoids the difficulties created by postulating the existence of things-in-themselves. It eliminates all scepticism, and makes knowledge not only possible but fully self-contained, liberating it from that mysterious, chaotic, and illusory 'outside world', belief in which had led both Hume and Kant to their erroneous conclusions. In Fichte's doctrine everything, as he put it, hangs firmly 'in a single ring, which is fastened to nothing, but maintains itself and the whole system by its own power'. This extension and modification of Kant's philosophy which started as an attempt to eliminate the imperfections of the *Critique of Pure Reason*, radically transformed some of the main problems of European philosophy as they were known since Descartes. These problems concerned causality, our knowledge of the external world, the relation of reason to sense-impressions and of mind to matter. On this new doctrine, however, philosophy became, to use the title of Hegel's[1] treatise, a phenomenology of Spirit, a

[1] It may be asked why this is the only mention of Hegel in this book. The explanation is simple: in spite of the sinister reputation which some writers have made for him, Hegel is not a nationalist, much less a precursor of Nazism. His political thought is concerned

science, that is, which investigates the workings of the universal consciousness, the order and character of its various manifestations. The poet Coleridge sums up in a few verses the vision of the universe which this philosophy tried to communicate:

> But what if all of animated nature
> Be but organic harps diversely framed,
> That tremble into thought, as o'er them sweeps,
> Plastic and vast one intellectual breeze,
> At once, the Soul of each, and God of all.

A particular consequence of this view, highly relevant to politics, is that the whole is prior to, more important, and greater than all its parts. A world takes on reality and coherence because it is the product of a single consciousness, and its parts can exist at all and share in reality only by taking their place within this world. In Fichte's words, the universe 'is an organic whole, no part of which can exist without the existence of all the rest; it cannot have come gradually into being, but must have been there complete at any period when it existed at all'. Only reality can be known; and the only reality is the whole. Knowledge of the parts is illusory; no parts can be known by themselves, since they cannot exist on their own, outside a coherent and ordered whole. F. W. Schelling (1775–1854), a philosopher of this school, who started as Fichte's disciple, went so far as to say: 'Individuals are only phantoms like the spectrum. They

with the state, not the nation. In particular what he has to say on the relation between absolute liberty and terror (*Phenomenology of Spirit*, Ch. VI, Section B), and on the difference between ancient and modern states, and the existence in the latter of what he calls civil society mediating between state and individual (*Philosophy of Right*, Part 111, Section 2), would make him an anti-nationalist. This, however, is not the place to decide the issue between Hegel and his enemies.

are not modifications of the absolute substance, but merely imaginary apparitions.' To apply this doctrine to politics is to travel a very long way from natural rights and utility. Natural rights were the natural rights of the individual, and utility was what he considered useful; likewise freedom meant that the individual was free. But if individuals by themselves are unreal, then natural rights and utility became empty sounds, and freedom is no longer a simple word, with a short, concise, dictionary definition. In this new theory, freedom is, even more emphatically than in Kant, an internal state, a determination of the will according to self-imposed commands, since the theory holds that nothing outside consciousness can possibly exist. But individuals, as such, are phantoms; they gain reality in so far as they have a place in a whole. Consequently, the freedom of the individual, which is his self-realization, lies in identifying himself with the whole, belonging to which endows him with reality. Complete freedom means total absorption in the whole, and the story of human freedom consists in the progressive struggle to reach this end. From this metaphysics the post-Kantians deduced a theory of the state. The end of man is freedom, freedom is self-realization, and self-realization is complete absorption in the universal consciousness. The state therefore is not a collection of individuals who have come together in order to protect their own particular interests; the state is higher than the individual and comes before him. It is only when he and the state are one that the individual realizes his freedom. 'I want to be a human being,' declares Fichte in his *Foundations of Natural Law* (1796), 'it is the aim of the state fully to procure this right for man.' The state, Fichte also says, is an artistic institution and its purpose is culture. Culture is the process whereby man becomes really man, realizing himself in utmost plenitude, and it is this realization which is the perfect freedom. For these conclusions, we must not forget, are the outcome of a search for an adequate conception of individual freedom. It is anxiety to secure full individual freedom which led Fichte at the beginning of his career to champion the extremer claims of the French revolutionaries, and to write that curious book, *The Closed Commercial State* (1800), which tries to show that true individual freedom can be secured only in a state which regulates to the minutest detail the life of its citizens. The individual leads a full, free, satisfactory life only if he and the state are one; to quote from *The Elements of Politics* (1809) by the publicist Adam Müller (1779-1829), the state is 'the intimate association of all physical and spiritual needs, of the whole nation into a great, energetic, infinitely active and living whole'; again, the state is *'the totality of human affairs, their union into a living whole*. If we exclude for ever from this association even the most unimportant part of the human being, if we separate private life from public life even at only one point, then we can no longer perceive the state as a phenomenon of life, or as an idea.'

The individual, then, cannot be considered on his own. He forms part of, and derives meaning from the whole. The image which has been commonly used to convey such an idea is that of the organism; and it is this image which Fichte himself uses in order to elucidate the relation between state and individual: 'The most exact image which may be used to explain this idea', he writes in *The Foundations of Natural Law*, 'is that of a product of organized nature, an idea which has been used lately with frequency in order to define the different branches of the public authority in its unity; but not yet, so far as I know, to explain the totality of civic relations. In a product of nature, no part is what it is but through its relation with the whole, and would absolutely not be what it is apart from this relation; more, if it had no organic relation at all it would be absolutely nothing, since without reciprocity in action between organic forces maintaining one another in equilibrium, no form would subsist, and a perpetual conflict between being and not-being would obtain, a conflict which would be unthinkable; similarly, man attains a determinate position in the scheme of things and fixity in nature only by means of civil association; he attains a particular position with regard to others and to nature only because he is in a particular association. . . . Between the isolated man and the citizen, there is the same relation as between raw and organized matter. . . . In an organized body, each part continuously maintains the whole, and in maintaining it, maintains itself also. Similarly, the citizen with regard to the state.' On such a view, the categorical imperative, obedience to which remained, according to Kant, the individual's sole responsibility, to be shared with or shifted on to nobody else, itself became possible and conceivable only through society. Society was the essential precondition of all laws of morality.

This theory, it may be said, has some affinities with Rousseau's political thought. Rousseau had also argued that neither individual nor state could attain happiness or virtue unless man exchanged a general will for his own selfish particular will, and willed the good of all, rather than his own. The affinity becomes even more striking when we read Rousseau's advice to the Poles on the reform of their government, which he penned in 1772. Here Rousseau insists that if a state is to be cohesive and lasting men must be trained to obey the law, not because they feel it is their duty or their interest to do so, but because they cannot desire or will anything which the laws do not prescribe; the laws then have, as he put it, 'the internal assent of their will'. Only then does the state cease to be a battleground of particular and contradictory interests; only then will it inspire absolute loyalty in the citizens, and will be reversed that 'execrable maxim' to the effect that where a man's good is, there is his fatherland – the very maxim which Goethe, as we have seen, was precisely then commending to his readers. But Rousseau was no metaphysician, no system-builder; his erratic. brilliant guesses, great though their influence was on Kant and Fichte, remained fragments, and did not constitute that whole which Fichte likened to 'a single ring, which is fastened to nothing' and which for him constituted the only true knowledge. Rousseau, then, does not provide a complete and rounded theory of the state, a theory which embraces first and last things, and which can proceed only from a unified and systematic vision of the universe. For this we have to go to the post-Kantians.

It has been a common feature of the European intellectual tradition to separate the life of action from the contemplative life, and to consider politics, which falls within the life of action, as an entirely practical pursuit. In despotisms politics meant skill in the manipulation of power, and in free governments it meant the practice of distributive justice, so that those fit to rule did in fact rule. Contemplation, on the other hand, was alien to, and perhaps quite subversive of, politics. The philosopher who spent his days trying to behold eternity, the mystic whose only desire was to lose himself in God, were of necessity withdrawn from and contemptuous of politics. But this new theory of the state reversed the traditional view: far from the life of action and the contemplative life being opposites, it was now held that the end of politics and the vocation of all citizens was that absorption into the universal consciousness which hitherto had been the ambition only of a few philosophers and mystics. Why, it may be asked, did philosophers begin to entertain such extravagant hopes and expect so much from political life? Was it merely that they were following through the conclusions of a metaphysics which they had no option but to accept? But, we must observe, the metaphysics did not make it strictly necessary to exalt the state so high, and make it the engine of individual salvation. These post-Kantian philosophers could well have argued, in the traditional manner,[2] that the fulfilment of man's destiny, that absorption in the whole, had nothing to do with the state, that, in fact, political life hindered rather than helped the quest. Besides, we can detect in what they have to say about the state a violence, an emotion, which may indicate that more is at issue than mere philosophical conclusions. 'What has become of the fables of ancient sages about the state?' laments Schleiermacher in his *Soliloquies*, 'Where is the power with which this highest level of existence should endow mankind, where the consciousness each should have of partaking in the state's reason, its imagination and its strength? Where is devotion to this new existence that man has conceived, a will to sacrifice the old individual soul rather than lose the state, a readiness to set one's life at stake rather than see the fatherland perish? Where is foresight keeping close watch lest the country be seduced and its spirit corrupted? Where find the individual character each state should have, and the acts that reveal it?'

[2] 'The philosopher sees that he has no ally with whose aid he might go and defend the right with a chance of safety. He is like a man in a den of wild beasts. Share their injustice he will not. He is not strong enough to hold out alone where all are savages. He would lose his life before he could do any benefit to the city or his friends and so be equally useless to himself and to the world. Weighing all these considerations he holds his peace and does his own work, like a man in a storm sheltering behind a wall from the driving wind of dust and hail.' Plato, *The Republic*, 496.

Why, it may be asked, these accents of intimate desolation, which a theologian should have reserved for spiritual, rather than worldly, alienation? 'A state, which constantly seeks to increase its internal strength', insists Fichte in his lectures on *The Characteristics of the Present Age* (1806), 'is thus forced to desire the gradual abolition. of all Favouritisms, and the establishment of Equal Rights for all men, in order that it, the state itself, may enter upon its own true Right – *to apply the whole surplus power of all its citizens, without exception, for the furtherance of its own purposes.*' This insistence that all favouritism be abolished, this yearning that the state should utilize the powers and capacities of all citizens without exception, provide a clue to the reason why this philosophy allowed politics such an exalted place.

When Fichte, Schleiermacher, and their fellow-writers described what the state ought to be and how far reality fell short of the vision, they had before their eyes the conditions in Prussia and the numerous other states of Germany. The rulers of these states were absolute. The best of them, and notably Frederick the Great, prided themselves on the efficient running of their administrative machinery, and on the existence in their domain of impersonal and expeditious justice, while the worst were capricious despots, spendthrift, improvident, and inefficient. German society everywhere was rigidly stratified into hidebound castes which looked upon each other with contempt or envy, and movement between which was extremely difficult. The writers who invented and elaborated the post-Kantian theory of the state belonged to a caste which was relatively low on the social scale. They were, most of them, the sons of pastors, artisans, or small farmers. They somehow managed to become university students, most often in the faculty of theology, and last out the duration of their course on minute grants, private lessons, and similar makeshifts. When they graduated they found that their knowledge opened no doors, that they were still in the same social class, looked down upon by a nobility which was stupid, unlettered, and which engrossed the public employments they felt themselves so capable of filling. These students and ex-students felt in them the power to do great things, they had culture, knowledge, ability, they yearned for the life of action, its excitements and rewards, and yet there they were, doomed to spend heartbreaking years as indigent curates waiting to be appointed pastors, or as tutors in some noble household, where they were little better than superior domestics, or as famished writers dependent on the goodwill of an editor or a publisher. Consider the pathetic outpourings of Johann Gottfried Herder (1744–1803) in the diary which he kept on his journey to France in 1769: 'Noble young man! All this waits asleep in you? But yet unfulfilled and neglected? Your low origin, the enslavement of your fatherland, your century's taste for trifles, the vicissitudes of your career have so limited you, have brought you so low that you cannot recognize yourself.' He feels it in him to be the equal of Lycurgus and Solon, to become the reformer of Livonia, where he had settled; if only he had the opportunity, he would convince the Governor-General of the province, and even become the favourite of the Empress of Russia. But what in fact is he? A pedagogue of uncertain prospects, involved in some ridiculous literary controversies. Such a situation goes far to explain Fichte's emphasis that in a well-run state all favouritism should disappear, that all citizens should be allowed to devote their powers and their talents to the greatness of the state.

To these men, society as it was then constituted seemed a cold, heartless place. They who knew themselves to be full of life and sparkle, of intelligence and originality, were being suffocated in the provincial, narrow, philistine society of the German principalities, or of a Prussia which for all its official enlightenment was, at bottom, dependent on the harsh will of a strict master. 'How unavailing', laments Schleiermacher in his *Soliloquies*, 'is the struggle of a superior mind, seeking moral cultivation and development, with this world that recognizes only legality, that offers dead formulas in place of life, custom and routine in place of free activity.' Men in their mutual relations, the state in its dealings with the subjects, paid regard not to the whole man, but to superficial qualities; they respected not intelligence but cleverness, they appreciated not inner cultivation but outer riches. No wonder then that young men grew stunted and deformed, their spirit bowed down and enslaved by rules and conventions. In his *Letters on the Aesthetic Education of Man* (1795), the dramatist Friedrich Schiller (1759–1805) draws up the indictment of a state which crushes with its lifeless weight spirit and liveliness in the individual, and transforms him into a machine. The disorder, he says, originated in the new learning in Europe, which delighted in dissecting, analysing, atomizing the whole man. This new learning fashions in its image the idea of the state; government becomes a common and clumsy mechanism, which is only fit to classify men in rough and ready categories; humanity is thus received at second hand, and is felt not as a living reality, but as 'a composition of intellect'. With a plangent, nostalgic eloquence, he describes the present sorry state of Europe: 'That polypus nature of the Grecian states, where each individual enjoyed an independent existence, and, in case of need, could act with the whole, now gives place to an ingenious enginery, in which a mechanical life forms itself as a whole, from the

patchwork of innumerable but lifeless parts. The state
and church, laws and customs, are now rent asunder;
enjoyment is separated from labour, the means from the
end, exertion from recompense. Eternally fettered only
to a single little fragment of the whole, man fashions
himself only as a fragment; ever hearing only the
monotonous whirl of the wheel which he turns, he
never displays the full harmony of his being, and,
instead of coining the humanity that is in his nature, he
is content with a mere impression of his occupation, his
science. . . . The dead letter represents the living intellect, and a hackneyed memory is a safer guide than
genius and feeling.' This could not continue. The illness
of society had to be cured. And the cure would be
effected only when men of intelligence and sensibility
were no longer left outside, when they were taken in
and given their rightful place. Such a cure, these writers
thought, only the state could effect. It was natural for
them to think that action by the state could and ought
to remove these obstacles; for they had before their very
eyes the mercantilist and absolutist state from whose
control and regulation no aspect of life, no social
activity, was immune. The state clearly was the source
of evil and good. Again, though they yearned for the life
of action, for positions and responsibilities, these men
were still, whether they liked it or not, academics and
intellectuals versed in the arguments of logic and
theology, but with little conception of political power,
or of administrative problems. This created a remarkable gulf between political speculation and political
practice which was no doubt also responsible for the
extravagant hopes of spiritual fulfilment which they set
on the state. 'Have we many dukes, grafen, or milords
among the writers of our nation?' asks a correspondent
of the periodical *Teutscher Merkur* in 1779. 'With us it
is candidates in Theology who treat of the interests of

the state, of commerce and of industry.' The candidates in theology, as has been seen, claimed for the state more than any absolutists had ever claimed. But was it really in the power of the state to grant them their wish, to banish the alienation, to still the discord between the inner and the outer man, and institute that harmonious life which, they believed, had once obtained in ancient Greece or medieval Christendom? For this is what they really wanted; it is to such a conclusion that their criticism of the lifeless enginery of enlightened Absolutism ultimately led. The evil could not be remedied, Adam Müller declared, 'so long as state and citizen serve two masters . . . so long as hearts are internally rent by a double desire, the *one* to live as a citizen in a state . . . the *other*, to extract himself from the whole civil order, to cut himself off from that same state along with his domestic and private life and with his most sacred feelings, indeed even with religion'. A state, says Schelling, 'constituted with a view to an external end, perhaps only in order to ensure mutual assurance of rights' is one based on compulsion and need; whereas in the true state 'science, religion and art become one, in living fashion, interpenetrating and becoming objective in their unity'. And in his celebrated *Addresses to the German Nation* (1807–8) Fichte scornfully rejected a state which merely maintained 'internal peace and a condition of affairs in which everyone may by diligence earn his daily bread and satisfy the needs of his material existence so long as God permits him to live'. 'All this', Fichte goes on to say, 'is only a means, a condition, and a framework for what love of fatherland really wants to bring about, namely, that the eternal and the divine may blossom in the world and never cease to become more and more pure, perfect and excellent.' This then is the full extent of the claim: that the state should be the creator of man's freedom not in an external and material sense, but in an internal and spiritual sense.

The phraseology of this theory of the state tends to disguise the element of violence that accompanies all government. Individuals, the theory says, merge their will in the will of the state, and in this merging they find freedom. They not only obey, but give their active assent to the laws and actions of the state. Force in such a case is irrelevant. But this is the case of the perfect state. If, however, such a phraseology were applied to the less perfect state, the effect would be to hide under soft euphemisms the hard issues of power which, by its very nature, is exercised by some over others. This phraseology would describe political matters in terms of development, fulfilment, self-determination, self-realization, and they would then be indistinguishable from aesthetic or religious questions where power is not in question. But if, as in actual states, government implies the existence of the hangman and the soldier, then to clothe issues of power in religious or aesthetic terminology can lead to a misleading and dangerous confusion. Reason of state begins to partake of sovereign Reason, and necessity of state to seem a necessity for eternal salvation.

This confusion between public and private, this intermixture between the spiritual and the temporal, has passed into current political rhetoric; and rulers have tried to persuade the ruled that relations between citizens are the same as those between lovers, husbands and wives, or parents and children, and that the bond uniting the individual to the state is religious, similar to that which unites the believer and his God, the prophet and his followers, or the mystic and his disciples. A speech by the Coptic leader of the Egyptian Wafd, Makram Ubaid, may illustrate this modern branch of rhetoric: 'The logic of the hear', Makram Ubaid declares, 'is love, and love is the foundation of all virtues. Love is one, however numerous its varieties and names. The love of God is religion, the love of virtue is good behaviour, the love of the fatherland is patriotism, the love of the family is kin-feeling, sexual love has been usually called love proper or amorousness, and the love of a friend is friendship. Thus, all feelings are gathered into one, which is love; their origin is one, and this is the heart; the heart is from God, and God is love as it is said in the Bible. . . .

'The feeling of love is essentially a mingling of souls. Love may be private, and in it would be included love of family, and love of friend; or it may be public, and this is love of the fatherland, or of religion, etc. Do not think that public love is a mere imaginary feeling. Nay, sometimes, especially at times of enthusiasm, its effect on the heart is even more powerful and more extensive than private love. Man may even sacrifice private love for the sake of public love, he may sacrifice his interests and his children for the sake of the love of his country, or for the sake of an exalted idea which has taken hold of him.' 'The love of the Egyptian for his brother-Egyptian in these last years', he continues, referring to the anti-British struggle at the end of the First World War, 'is not mere patriotic feeling; it is rather the love of the believer for his fellow-believer, for all believers are brothers,[3] it is the love of the soldier for his fellow-soldier—it is therefore a strong love, concentrated into one idea, one army and one leader. This love has possessed our sons, and for its sake they have shed their blood and sacrificed their freedom. . . .

'The best description of this public love occurs in the revealed Scriptures, where it is said that those who share a common belief and a common idea, are brethren and kin. Up to now, I used to be greatly surprised when

[3] Textual quotation from the Qur'an, XLIX: 9.

I read in the Gospels that when Christ was told "Your mother and brethren are without desiring to speak with you", he replied in a vehement tone to the effect that his mother and brethren and relatives were those who were at one with him in right ideas and good works[4] – yes! These are the true kin, those who are bound by spiritual, not carnal bonds!'

This exaltation of the state also exalts the philosopher, the academic. He ceases to be the reflective man in whom understanding necessarily precludes action; he is no longer only a scholar who advances knowledge or a teacher of youth who guards and transmits the heritage; he now claims to be the true legislator of the human race. Politics on this view is intimately bound up with man's ultimate destiny; understanding, therefore, and action are not opposites. Understanding is understanding of the whole, and right action is action which tends to absorption in the whole. Action is understanding, and understanding action. 'The Scholar', writes Fichte in *The Vocation of the Scholar* (1794), 'sees not merely the present – he sees also the future: he sees not merely the point which humanity now occupies, but also that to which it must next advance. . . . In this respect, the Scholar is the *Guide* of the human race.' This large claim does not withstand sober scrutiny, but it came, in time, to be widely accepted in Europe and beyond. The veneration which Antiquity gave to legislators and founders of cities was now bestowed on publicists and professors; erudite philologists, or abstruse and complicated economists became the acknowledged founders of powerful political movements, drawing their inspiration from the uncouth vocabulary of philosophical controversies. The necessary concomittant of such a

[4] The speaker here adapts to his purposes St Matthew, XII: 46–50.

situation is an ideological style of politics. Interest, expediency, or the necessities of the case are not sufficient to justify political action. A metaphysical system must provide, from the outside, the norms of political behaviour, and a constant effort must take place in order to reconcile actions with first principles. To men established in power, this may be no more than a useful formality which, however, ends by widening the gulf between what is said and what is done, thereby corrupting the vocabulary of politics. By means of high philosophical words rulers can better control the ruled, who are ensnared by their literacy, and obtain their active support or their passive acquiescence. Thus, by a natural development, it is not philosophers who become kings, but kings who tame philosophy to their use. Such a political style calls forth a new class of literature: a Lenin discourses on empirio-criticism, and a Stalin expounds the principles of philology; a Hitler in-augurates his career with a *Mein Kampf*, while an Abd al-Nasir crowns a successful *coup d'état* with a *Philosophy of the Revolution.*

4

THE EXCELLENCE OF DIVERSITY

THE destiny of man is accomplished, and his freedom realized by absorption within the state, because only through the state does he attain coherence and acquire reality. It might, then, seem logical to conclude that such a state should embrace the whole of humanity. But this would be, nonetheless, erroneous, for it would conflict with another, essential feature of this metaphysic, namely, that self-realization and absorption into the whole is not a smooth, uneventful process, but the outcome of strife and struggle. Struggle, as has been seen, is a concomitant of Kant's ethical theory: the free, autonomous man becomes such only by striving against the heteronomous natural inclinations. But this was not the only reason why the post-Kantians thought struggle so prominent a feature of the world.

Any philosophy worth considering must attempt to account for the existence of evil in the world. But the philosophy of the Enlightenment, which had discarded innate ideas and the orthodox religious account of the Creation, found it extremely difficult to make place for evil in its scheme, let alone to account for it. For if all knowledge and morality were based on sensations, and derived from man's natural environment, then no action was, properly speaking, evil, and yet evil was there, not to be ignored or blinked. What, then, was its function in the economy of the world? Here came to be appreciated what C. L. Becker has called the uses of posterity.[1] The progress of mankind was manifest. It had advanced in knowledge and science, it was gradually shedding its superstitions and daily becoming happier and more civilized. To explain evil was then quite easy. Evil was necessary in the passage from barbarity to civilization, from ignorance to knowledge. This change was effected only through struggle, violence, upheavals. The justification of evil lay in the future, when our descendants would enjoy the blessings which our sufferings made possible. Evil was, that good might ensue: 'It is only through turmoil and destruction,' said Turgot in his lecture of 1750 *On the Successive Advances of the Human Mind*, 'that nations expand, that civilization and governments are in the long run perfected.' For if there had been no tumultuous and dangerous passions, there would be no progress and mankind would remain in a state of mediocrity. For Kant, this idea was a fundamental one. He explicitly looked on history as a ceaseless struggle. Good and evil, he wrote in his essay *Of the Different Human Races* (1775-7), were inextricably mixed in man, and constitute the source of energy for those 'great springs which put into motion the creative forces of humanity and compel it to develop all its talents, and to aspire to the perfection of its destiny'. Left to himself, he says in his *Idea of a Universal History on a Cosmopolitical Plan* (1784), man would choose peace; but Nature wills otherwise: for the good of his species war must be his lot. Only through war will man attain the life of Reason. Individuals may pursue this or that end, agitate themselves in their own puny concerns; in spite of themselves, they contribute to Nature's plan which will

---

[1] In The Heavenly City of the Eighteenth Century Philosophers, New Haven, 1932.

be manifest only in the last generations when humanity will at last become both virtuous and happy. Such a theory attributes to nature and history a blind, impersonal urge towards the fulfilment of morality, and is thus, on the face of it, inconsistent with Kant's ethical doctrine which ascribes morality only to the conscious action of the self-determining, autonomous individual. But Kant, nonetheless, never ceased to allow a central place for the notion of struggle in his philosophy of history. In the treatise on *Perpetual Peace* which he published in 1794, he rejected the prospect of a universal monarchy. It is true that such a monarchy might establish peace, but it would be the peace of despotism, and to this even war was rationally preferable. In any case, nature does not allow the establishment of a universal monarchy: 'She employs two means to separate peoples and to prevent them from mixing: differences of language and of religion. These differences involve a tendency to mutual hatred and pretexts for war, but the progress of civilization and men's gradual approach to greater harmony in their principles finally leads to peaceful agreement. This is not that peace which despotism (in the burial ground of freedom) produces through a weakening of all powers; it is, on the contrary, produced and maintained by their equilibrium in liveliest competition.' The nature of the world, then, the course and the fulfilment of history alike, prevented the existence of a universal state. The world must be a world of many states.

Fichte exalted further the idea of struggle. The world, it has been seen, is a product of the Ego's consciousness. The Ego bodies forth the world, with all its rawness and imperfection, not for its own sake, but in order to have an antagonist. Without opposition or struggle the Ego would not be able to attain consciousness of itself, and no moral life would then be possible. The shock resulting from the opposition of the Ego and the world, so to say, arouses the Ego to endeavour self-realization. This endeavour is infinite and ceaseless; should perfection at last be realized, and striving come to a stop, all activity ends and death results. In this theory, struggle assumes such importance that the world itself exists only in order to make it possible. In the philosophy of history which he put forward in *The Characteristics of the Present Age*, Fichte maintained the central position of the idea of struggle. War between states he regards as that mechanism which introduces 'a living and progressive principle into History'; and this war is not the limited war, the decorous game of chess of eighteenth-century strategy; it is, he says, 'a true and proper war – a war of subjugation'. This conflict between states promotes indirectly the self-realization of the whole human race: 'So long as Humanity received but a one-sided culture in different states, it was to be expected that each particular state should deem its own culture the true and only civilization, and regard that of other states as mere Barbarism, and their inhabitants as savages – and thus feel itself called upon to subdue them.' In this manner, humanity gradually ascends the scale of culture, and its highest point at any particular time is to be found in that state which, for the moment, is victorious over its rivals. For this reason Fichte maintained, in this work, that one should not regret the decline of one's own country in the course of the struggle; our true Fatherland must always be that state which occupies 'the highest rank of culture'.

This philosophy of history and of the state was however modified by another element which combined with the idea of self-determination, of individual fulfilment through absorption in the state, and of struggle, as the essential process both in nature and history, to produce the doctrine of nationalism as we now know it. This new element was principally contributed by Herder, and is to be found set out mainly in two of his works, *Another Philosophy of History* (1774), a short pamphlet of indignant eloquence, and the much longer *Outlines of a Philosophy of the History of Man*, published over a period from 1784 to 1791, a large and diffuse, hut original and powerful, attempt at universal history in the most comprehensive sense. Herder did accept the two prevalent ideas of the philosophy of history of his age, namely, that the historical process was one of progressive amelioration, and that improvement was the outcome of violence and struggle. On these points he was as emphatic as any. Violence and revolutions fill history, wreck upon wreck. But in compensation there is a chain of improvement linking the whole history of man. Improvement itself, however, requires that man should build nothing lasting: 'Folly must appear, that wisdom might surmount it: decaying fragility even of the noblest works was an essential property of their materials, that men might have an opportunity of exerting fresh labours in improving or building upon their ruins: for we are all here in a state of exercise.' And even more eloquently: 'Only amid storms can the noble plant flourish: only by opposing struggle against false pretensions can the sweet labours of man be victorious. Nay men frequently appear to sink under their honest purposes: but it is only in appearance: the seed germinates more beautifully in a subsequent period from the ashes of the good, and when irrigated with blood seldom fails to shoot up to an unfading flower.' But Herder rebelled against the complacent belief, which he attributed to French and Frenchified writers, that the age in which they happened to be living was the most excellcnt one, for which all the previous centuries had been merely a preparation. This attitude systematically belittled and depreciated all the achievements of the past. He himself rejected this teleological arrogance: there was indeed progress, but the achievements of the past were not merely means to the end that Voltaire might at last manifest himself to a grateful humanity. These achievements had an intrinsic worth on their own, and no particular one might be depreciated, so that another might be exalted. 'All the works of God,' he argued, 'have this property, that although they belong to a whole, which no eye can scan, each is in itself a whole, and bears the divine character of its destination. It is so with the brute, and the plant: can it be otherwise with man? Can it be, that thousands are made for one? all the generations that have passed away, merely for the last? every individual only for the Species, that is for the image of an abstract name? The Allwise sports not in this manner: he invents no finespun shadowy dreams: he lives and feels in each of his children with paternal affection, as though it were the only creature in the world. All his means are ends: all his ends are means to higher ends, in which the Infinite, filling all, reveals himself.' Diversity, then, as much as struggle, is a fundamental characteristic of the universe. Diversity and not uniformity is worthy of notice, because diversity is patently the design of God. This is made plain if we consider that God has scattered men all over the globe, and has exposed them to various climates and environments. He must have willed that all the possible varieties of creation should have a chance to live and realize themselves in their own individual, peculiar, idiosyncratic fashion; as Schiller for his part put it in his *Philosophical Letters* (1786-9): 'Every kind of perfection must attain existence in the fullness of the world. . . . Every offspring of the brain, everything that wit can fashion, has an unchallengeable right of citizenship in this larger understanding of the creation.

In the infinite chasm of Nature no activity can be
omitted, no grade of enjoyment be wanting in the
universal happiness. . . . In the work of the Divine
Artist, the unique value of each part is respected, and
the sustaining gaze with which he honours every spark
of energy in even the lowliest creature manifests his
glory not less than the harmony of the immeasurable
whole.'

Not only, then, is the world as it is imperfect, and
struggling for perfection. This eventual perfection,
when it comes, will be a harmony of all the possible
varieties of creatures which Nature or God can bring
forth. In this diversitarian view of the world, spontaneity rather than imitation is given first preference,
and a change comes over the accepted idea of Nature. In
the system of Natural Law, the idea of Nature meant
regularity, uniformity, maturity, and finish. But
regularity and uniformity imply imitation, imitation
implies artifice, and artifice is, on the diversitarian view,
unspontaneous, hence unnatural. Nature now connotes
that which disregards symmetry and balance, that
which rejects any suggestion of the contrived, of the
consciously arranged, that which is raw, rough, and
immature. And spontaneity is the gift of those who
retain their own peculiar character, who are not
corrupted by the veneer of civilization; while those who
do not cherish their own individuality, who move from
one culture to another, from one civilization to another,
are homeless parasites, doomed to artificiality and
sterility. 'The savage', says Herder, 'who loves himself,
his wife, and child, with quiet joy, and glows with
limited activity for his tribe as for his own life, is, in my
opinion, a more real being than that cultivated shadow,
who is enraptured with the love of the shades of his
whole species, that is of a name. The savage has room in
his hut for every stranger, whom he receives as his

brother with calm benevolence, and asks not whence he comes. The deluged heart of the idle cosmopolite is a hut for no-one.'

This emphasis on diversity was but taking up and somewhat modifying a traditional idea which, as A. 0. Lovejoy showed in his classic work, *The Great Chain of Being* (1936), has been a main theme in European thought since Plato's day. Diversity, many writers had previously argued, was a necessary feature of the Creation, because God could not have willed, in His infinite goodness, to deny life to any possible species of creature, however mean or insignificant. In this latest variant of the argument, diversity, which is willed by God, came to mean not only that every culture, every individuality, has a unique incomparable value, but also that there is a duty laid upon us to cultivate our own peculiar qualities and not mix or merge them with others. Only thus can we act morally and further the progress of the world. 'Only if man is conscious of his individuality in his present conduct', argues Schleiermacher, 'can he be sure of not violating it in his next act, and only if he requires himself constantly to survey the whole of humanity, opposing his own expression of it to every other possible one, can he maintain the consciousness of his unique selfhood.' This view, applied to politics, drastically alters the idea of nation. A nation, to the French revolutionaries, meant a number of individuals who have signified their will as to the manner of their government. A nation, on this vastly different theory, becomes a natural division of the human race, endowed by God with its own character, which its citizens must, as a duty, preserve pure and inviolable. Since God has separated the nations, they should not be amalgamated. 'Every nationality', proclaims Schleiermacher, 'is destined through its peculiar organization and its place in the world to represent a certain side of the divine image. . . . For it is God who directly assigns to each nationality its definite task on earth and inspires it with a definite spirit in order to glorify Himself through each one in a peculiar manner.' Nations are separate natural entities ordained by God, and the best political arrangement obtains when each nation forms a state on its own. The true and lasting state is one where a nation is formed through natural kinship and affection. States in which there is more than one nation, on the other hand, are unnatural, oppressive, and finally doomed to decay. Herder's argument here is not so much that in such states one element may dominate the others; rather, that they sin against the principle of diversity, for in them the different nations always run the risk of losing their identity, and are not able fully to cultivate their originality. That this is his dominant thought appears from the examples he chooses to illustrate his argument. The empire of the Ottomans and the Grand Mogul are corrupt states which comprise a multitude of nations; while the states of China, of the Brahmins, and of the Jews are wholesome states which, even if they perish, leave the nation intact, because it has been able to withstand intermixture with other nations. It follows on this that the member of one nation must not take up the customs or the language of another nation. Such a man forsakes the spontaneous and the genuine and embraces the contrived and the artificial. He thus impoverishes his nation and hinders the assertion of its individuality.

'Look at other nationalities,' cries Herder in a poem 'To the Germans':

> Do they wander about
> So that nowhere in the whole world they are strangers
> Except to themselves?
> They regard foreign countries with proud disdain.

And you German alone, returning from abroad,
Wouldst greet your mother in French?
O spew it out, before your door
Spew out the ugly slime of the Seine
Speak German, O you German!

This heated language may seem merely to insist in an exaggerated manner on the duty, derived from the diversitarian principle, of cultivating and preserving one's own peculiar identity. For a German to speak French would be to imitate, to lose his spontaneity; worse, it would be to expose himself to a culture which rejected spontaneity, simplicity, sensuous feeling, and vigour, which preferred dead imitation, and a spurious neo-classicism. But we may appreciate this vehemence better if we realize that the objection to French was the outcome not only of a historical and literary theory but also proceeded from resentment at the intellectual's position in German society. In eighteenth-century Germany French was considered eminently the language of literature and of polite society. French writers basked in the patronage of Frederick the Great, who did not hide his contempt for German literature and German writers. In these, resentment against their lowly position became confounded with resentment against the French language and French literature which the privileged classes and their imitators affected to cultivate. It was literary men, with literary preoccupations, who thus endowed language with political significance. The publicist and nationalist agitator Ernst Moritz Arndt (1769-1860), in his memoirs published in 1840, recalls with triumphant contempt that in the last decades of the eighteenth century even farmers' daughters in his small North German town affected to converse in French: 'Scraps of French were thrown in, too, every now and then, and I remember my amusement when I began to learn the language, at recognizing the "fladrun" (*flacon*) as Fraulein B—— used to call her water bottle, and the Wun Schur (*bonjour*) and à la Wundör (*à la bonne heure!*) and similar flourishes with which on their rides, the huntsmen and farmers used to greet one another when they wished to be particularly elegant.' This French mania seemed to these writers another aspect of the superficiality and decadence of those set in authority over them. 'Already all the European princes', exclaims Herder, bitterly ironical, in *Another Philosophy of History*, 'and soon we too will speak in French. And then – oh happiness! the golden age will begin anew.' '"The whole earth,"' he writes, quoting Scripture '"was of one language and of one speech," "and there shall be one fold and one shepherd !" O national characters, what has become of you?' Cultured persons might scoff at people simple enough to remain content with their own customs and prejudices; but it is these which preserve the health and sturdiness of society. The first signs of social sickness reveal themselves when people begin to yearn for foreign travel, to admire foreign things and despise their own. Later, after the Napoleonic invasion, when the Prussian state fell apart and Frederick's military and administrative machine was discredited, the cry went up that the evil was caused by the French influence and the corruption in which it resulted. Francophobia may well have started as a theory of literature; it was difficult, in the end, to distinguish it from a political crusade. The agitator Friedrich Jahn (1778-1852) could cry out at a public meeting in Berlin that he who allowed his daughter to learn French was delivering her up to prostitution, and Arndt, in a pamphlet of 1818, could exclaim: 'Let us hate the French strongly, and let us hate our own French who dishonour and ravage our energy and our innocence.' By then, such an assertion had an intricate theory to support it, which proclaimed the intimate and fateful link between language and politics.

5

NATIONAL SELF-
DETERMINATION

FROM the principle of diversity it follows, as has been seen, that the peculiarities, the idiosyncrasies, the differences which distinguish individuals from one another are things holy, to be fostered and preserved, since only through each individual cultivating his own peculiarity, through each different species reaching the perfection of its kind, can the universal harmony be attained. Language is the means through which a man becomes conscious of his personality. Language is not only a vehicle for rational propositions, it is the outer expression of an inner experience, the outcome of a particular history, the legacy of a distinctive tradition. In a prize essay of 1772, the *Treatise upon the Origin of Language*, Herder argued in a subtle and forceful manner against the theories of speech current in his day. He rejected the view that each language was a special creation of God, that language is a product of the rational faculty, or that language originated in the onomatopoeic ejaculations of primitive man. Man is no passive spectator of the world; he is, on the contrary, actively involved in what he observes or experiences, and language was born as man tried to express his feelings towards the things and events which he came across. Language is originally neither description nor imitation; rather it is a living amalgam in which things and happenings are combined with the emotions which

they arouse in man: 'As man referred everything to
himself, because everything seemed to speak to him,
and really acted either for or against him, he took part
either with or against it, loved or hated it, and repre-
senting everything to himself, in a human manner, all
the traces of human nature must have impressed
themselves upon the first denominations. They therefore pronounced love or hatred, curse or blessing,
interest or dislike, and the articles more especially have
in many languages originated from this feeling.
Everything became personified in a human manner, as
male and female, everywhere Gods and Goddesses,
beneficent or malicious active beings, the roaring storm,
the gentle Zephyr, the limpid spring, the boisterous
ocean, their whole mythology lies in these rich mines, in
the verbs and nouns of ancient languages, and the oldest
dictionary was a resounding Pantheon, a place of
assemblage for both sexes, according as nature revealed
herself to the senses of the first discoverer.' Man's
earliest language, then, derives from the senses and it is
only later that abstract words are invented; but these
words are solidly based on a substratum of sensual
impressions and reactions. Since, also, men have not
continued one flock, but have dispersed over all the
earth, and have divided into distinct families, tribes, and
nations, their languages bear the imprint of their
varying circumstances and distinct identities. 'Only one
language', says Schleiermacher, 'is firmly implanted in
an individual. Only to one does he belong entirely, no
matter how many he learns subsequently . . . For every
language is a particular mode of thought and what is
cogitated in one language can never be repeated in the
same way in another. . . . Language, thus, just like the
church or the state, is an expression of a peculiar life
which contains within it and develops through it a
common body of language.'

This theory has had immense political consequences. The world is a world of diversity, and humanity is divided into nations. Language is the external and visible badge of those differences which distinguish one nation from another; it is the most important criterion by which a nation is recognized to exist, and to have the right to form a state on its own. So crucial is the linguistic criterion that Fichte in his *Addresses to the German Nation* goes so far as to say that 'we give the name of people to men whose organs of speech are influenced by the same external conditions, who live together, and who develop their language in continuous communication with each other'. Fichte devotes a considerable portion of his *Addresses* to discovering and laying bare the intimate and complex relations between language and politics. Herder had argued that for a man to speak a foreign language was to live an artificial life, to be estranged from the spontaneous, instinctive sources of his personality. With great ingenuity, Fichte works out the political ramifications of this broad and general contention. He tries to show, for instance, that the mere presence of foreign vocables within a language can do great harm, by contaminating the very springs of political morality. When foreign terms relating to political and social life are introduced into a language, those who speak it are unsure of the exact connotations of those terms and they fall into confusions which can lead to great harm. Take for instance, he argues, the words Humanity, Popularity and Liberality. These words are of Latin origin, and were introduced into German as *Humanität*, *Popularität* and *Liberalität*. What does Humanity really mean? It means the quality of being a man, and in this there is nothing praiseworthy. But the Romans, because they had a low ethical standard, considered being a man praiseworthy. To introduce then the word *Humanität* into German is to introduce a low ethical standard among the German people. 'Now', he says, if instead of the word *Humanity* we had said to a German the word *Menschlichkeit*, which is its literal translation, he would have understood us without further historical explanation, but he would have said: "Well, to be a man (Mensch), and not a wild beast, is not very much after all." ' In similar fashion, Fichte deals with the words Popularity and Liberality, which, to him, only show the degradation of Roman political institutions. 'There is in the word Popularity,' he points out, 'even at the very beginning, something base, which was perverted (in the mouths of the Romans) and became a virtue, owing to the corruption of the nation and its constitution. The German,' on the other hand, 'never falls into this perversion, so long as it is put before him in his own language.' If, instead of introducing these three words into German, writers had confined themselves to proper German vocables, like *Menschenfreundlichkeit* (friendliness to man), *Leutseligkeit* (condescension or affability), and *Edelmuth* (noble-mindedness), the perversions implicit in the Latin terms would have remained unknown to the Germans.

If such is the harm which results from introducing a few foreign words into German, what must it be like when a people abandons its tongue and wholly adopts a foreign language? The French were originally Teutons who forsook German speech for a neo-Latin idiom. With the neo-Latin language came all the faults of the Romans, and the French now suffer, as Fichte puts it, 'from the idea of lack of seriousness about social relations, the idea of self-abandonment, and the idea of heartless laxity'. Had they retained their original speech they would never have allowed such degradation to befall them, for then they would have still possessed a living language, and would have been able, by means of it, to guard against the notions introduced and made popular by the use of Latin. Indeed, to look at the matter closely, Fichte asserts, those who speak neo-Latin languages do not, properly speaking, possess a living speech, a mother tongue; they merely make do with a dead language. Fichte's distinction between living and dead languages rests on the theory of the origin of language advanced by Herder in his treatise of 1772, to which currency was also given in the *Lectures on Literature and Art* delivered by A. W. Schlegel in 1803. Original, primitive languages, Fichte says, are superior to composite, derived languages. German is an original language, while French and English are composite, derived languages. Like Herder, Fichte argues that in any language abstract ideas are expressed in non-abstract terms, or, as he puts it, 'Language gives a sensuous image of the supersensuous'. Those who speak an original language maintain unbroken the connexion between the abstract ideas and the sense-experience which has given rise to the terms in which abstract ideas are expressed. 'To all who will but think', he says, speaking of those nations with original languages, 'the image deposited in the language is clear; to all who really think it is alive and stimulates their life,' and this, because 'from the time the first sound broke forth among the same people, (such a language) has developed continuously out of the actual common life of this people and . . . no element has ever entered (into it) that did not express an observation actually experienced by this people, and, moreover, an observation standing in a connexion of widespread reciprocal influence with the other observations of the same people.' The case is quite the opposite with those who speak a derived language. Here, the living connexion between abstract ideas and immediate sense-experience is severed – their personality is therefore impoverished, and they cannot attain freedom and fulfilment. For them 'the verbal image contains a comparison with an observation of the senses, which they have either passed over long ago without the accompanying mental development, or else have not yet had, and perhaps never can have . . . In this way they receive the flat and dead history of a foreign culture, but not in any way a culture of their own. They get symbols which for them are neither immediately clear nor able to stimulate life, but which must seem to them entirely as arbitrary as the sensuous part of the language.' For those, on the other hand, fortunate enough to have it, a primitive language 'does not exert an influence on life; it is itself the life of him who thinks in this fashion. . . . Just because that kind of thinking *is* life, it is felt by its possessor with inward pleasure in its vitalizing, transfiguring and liberating power.'

From this, two conclusions may be drawn: first, that people who speak an original language are nations, and second, that nations must speak an original language. To speak an original language is to be true to one's character, to maintain one's identity, and as German is an original language only the German escapes the artificiality and sterility of those who speak dead languages; and only the German, the original man who is not enmeshed in a lifeless, mechanical organization, considers Fichte, 'really has a people and is entitled to count on one, and he alone is capable of real and rational love for his nation'. Again, since a nation, *ipso facto*, must speak an original language, its speech must be cleansed of foreign accretions and borrowings, since the purer the language, the more natural it is, and the easier it becomes for the nation to realize itself, and to increase its freedom. All the more, therefore, is it incumbent on a nation worthy of the name, to revive, develop, and extend what is taken to be its original speech, even though it might be found only in remote villages, or had not been used for centuries, even though its resources are inadequate and its literature poor – for only such an original language will allow a nation to realize itself and attain freedom. Such is the doctrinal foundation of the vast philological labours which have accompanied the spread of nationalism all over the world; well might nationalists adopt the motto wittily coined by the historian Albert Sorel: 'I speak, therefore I am.'[1]

The test, then, by which a nation is known to exist is that of language. A group speaking the same language is known as a nation, and a nation ought to constitute a state. It is not merely that a group of people speaking a certain language may claim the right to preserve its language; rather, such a group, which is a nation, will cease to be one if it is not constituted into a state. Then, says Fichte, 'it is . . . bound to give up its language, and to coalesce with its conquerors, in order that there may be unity and internal peace and complete oblivion of relationships which no longer exist.' Such a group, absorbed in a foreign state, is doomed to death; its members become, in Fichte's eloquent metaphors, 'an appendix to the life which bestirred itself of its own accord before them or beside them; they are an echo resounding from the rock, an echo of a voice already silent; they are, considered as a people, outside the original people, and to the latter they are strangers and foreigners'. Again, if a nation is a group of people speaking the same language, then if political frontiers separate the members of such a group, these frontiers are arbitrary, unnatural, unjust. 'Understand me rightly,' says a character in Fichte's dialogue *Patriotism*

---

[1] A. Sorel, *L'Europe et la révolution française*, Vol. I, Paris, 1885, p. 429.

and its Opposite (1807), 'the separation of Prussians from the rest of the Germans is purely artificial. . . . The separation of the Germans from the other European nations is based on Nature. Through a common language and through common national characteristics which unite the Germans, they are separate from the others.' Only on this assumption did it make sense to entitle his lectures *Addresses to the German Nation*. For when they were delivered in Berlin in 1807-8 there was, politically, no German nation. The German-speaking parts of Europe had the most diverse political arrangements, and the fact that Prussians and Bavarians, Bohemians and Silesians all spoke German was not considered of great political moment, certainly not enough to warrant the disruption of so many settled institutions. Fichte and his fellow-nationalists strove to prove and convince that the fact of speaking one language was sufficient reason for upsetting all existing political arrangements, and for bringing about a new one in which all who spoke the German tongue would form part of the same state. 'What is the fatherland of the German?' asks Arndt in the well-known poem *The German Fatherland*. 'Name me the great country! Where the German tongue sounds and sings *lieder* in God's praise, that's what it ought to be. Call that thine, valiant German! . . . That is the fatherland of the German – where anger roots out foreign nonsense, where every Frenchman is called enemy, where every German is called friend – That is what it ought to be. It ought to be the whole of Germany!' The French Revolution, as has been seen, gave currency to the principle that individuals and communities have the right to secede from one and adhere to another state. No less revolutionary in its consequences is this other principle that the boundaries of states are natural, and correspond with the linguistic map of a territory. 'The

first, original, and truly national boundaries of a state',
lays down Fichte, 'are beyond doubt the internal
boundaries. Those who speak the same language are
joined to each other by a multitude of invisible bonds by
nature herself, long before any human art begins; they
understand each other and have the power to make
themselves understood more and more clearly; they
belong together and are by nature one and inseparable
whole. . . . From this internal boundary . . . the making
of the external boundary by dwelling place results as a
consequence; and in the natural view of things it is not
because men dwell between certain mountains and
rivers that they are a people, but, on the contrary, men
dwell together . . . because they were a people already
by a law of nature which is much higher.' A nation,
then, becomes a homogeneous linguistic mass which
acts as a magnet for groups speaking the same language
outside its boundaries, who are tempted to throw off
allegiance to their state, and embark on sedition and
civil war. Irredentism is a phenomenon which appears
following the propagation of nationalism. Again, if
states must be formed of linguistically homogeneous
nations, then in areas of mixed speech, the unity of the
national state is sorely disturbed; for, as Fichte points
out, 'such a whole (as the nation), if it wishes to absorb
and mingle with itself any other people of different
descent and language, cannot do so without itself
becoming confused . . . and violently disturbing the even
process of its culture.' This emphasis on language
transformed it into what it had seldom been before, into
a political issue for which men are ready to kill and
exterminate each other. The linguistic criterion also
makes extremely difficult the orderly functioning of a
society of states. For such a society to function, states
must be reasonably stable, well-defined entities, known
and recognized by the extent of territory they control,

by their clearly delimited frontiers, by the coercive power of which they dispose. If language becomes the criterion of statehood, the clarity essential to such a notion is dissolved in a mist of literary and academic speculation, and the way is open for equivocal claims and ambiguous situations. Such an outcome is inescapable with such a theory as nationalism, invented as it was by literary men who had never exercised power, and appreciated little the necessities and obligations incidental to intercourse between states. These men knew that the petty states which made up the Holy Roman Empire were intolerably confining and that change was imperative; also, their metaphysics – and they were metaphysicians first and foremost – did not incline them to value politics as a practical, prosaic activity, to heed Cicero's austere advice that if Sparta is your inheritance, you must make the best of her. Politics to them, was, rather, a golden key which gave entrance to fabled realms. But since politics usually deals with actual realms, nationalists must operate in a hazy region, midway between fable and reality, in which states, frontiers, compacts are at once both real and unreal. Egypt, for instance, is a state clearly recognizable within the society of states, having a defined territory ruled by a known sovereign authority able to negotiate and enter into agreements with other states. Yet, the head of this state, Abd al-Nasir, writes in his *Philosophy of the Revolution* (1954): 'If I were told that our place is the capital we live in I beg to differ. If I were told that our place is limited by the political boundaries of our country I also do not agree.' Such a view rejects the ordinary conventions and rules of an orderly society of states, but does nothing to provide a workable substitute.

It is sometimes argued that there are two or more varieties of nationalism, the linguistic being only one of a number, and the Nazi doctrine of race is brought forward to illustrate the argument that there can be racial, religious, and other nationalisms. But, in fact, there is no definite clear-cut distinction between linguistic and racial nationalism. Originally, the doctrine emphasized language as the test of nationality, because language was an outward sign of a group's peculiar identity and a significant means of ensuring its continuity. But a nation's language was peculiar to that nation only because such a nation constituted a racial stock distinct from that of other nations. The French nationalist writer, Charles Maurras (1868-1952), exemplified this connection between race and language when he remarked that no Jew, no Semite, could understand or handle the French language as well as a Frenchman proper; no Jew, he remarked, could appreciate the beauties of Racine's line in *Bérénice*: *'Dans l'orient désert quel devint mon ennui.'* It was then no accident that racial classifications were, at the same time, linguistic ones, and that the Nazis distinguished the members of the German Aryan race scattered in Central and Eastern Europe by a linguistic criterion. In doing this, the Nazis only simplified and debased the ideas implicit in the writings of Herder and others. Such ideas received great impetus during the nineteenth century owing to the development of ethnological studies. A writer like the Comte de Gobineau (1816 –82), for instance, worked out at great length and with great ingenuity and learning, a theory which he presented in his *Essay on the Inequality of the Human Races* (1853–5). According to him humanity was originally divided into three distinct races with different innate abilities: of these the white Aryan race was undoubtedly by far the most able, and, by mixing with the other races, it raised them up to civilization. Gobineau, it is interesting to note, explicitly argued that each race had its own natural language proper to it. It may be added that he himself considered the mingling of races as inevitable, as indeed the mechanism whereby civilization became possible; but he looked on the process with melancholy resignation, since the white Aryan race, having bestowed its excellences on the other races, was now exhausted, and the world was therefore bound to sink into degradation and, at last, to suffer extinction. 'What is sad to foresee', he wrote, 'is not death, it is the certainty that we will die degraded; and even such a shame which is reserved for our descendants, might leave us unmoved, were it not that we feel, with secret horror, that the rapacious hands of fate are already upon ourselves.' Such speculations the Nazis perverted to their own purposes, and made of them a weapon of persecution and terror.

In nationalist doctrine, language, race, culture, and sometimes even religion, constitute different aspects of the same primordial entity, the nation. The theory admits here of no great precision, and it is misplaced ingenuity to try and classify nationalisms according to the particular aspect which they choose to emphasize. What is beyond doubt is that the doctrine divides humanity into separate and distinct nations, claims that such nations must constitute sovereign states, and asserts that the members of a nation reach freedom and fulfilment by cultivating the peculiar identity of their own nation and by sinking their own persons in the greater whole of the nation. All these different facets of the doctrine are admirably summed up in an utterance of Schleiermacher's: 'How little worthy of respect', he exclaims, 'is the man who roams about hither and thither without the anchor of national ideal and love of fatherland; how dull is the friendship that rests merely upon personal similarities in disposition and tendencies, and not upon the feeling of a greater common unity for

whose sake one can offer up one's life; how the greatest
source of pride is lost by the woman that cannot feel
that she also bore children for her fatherland and
brought them up for it, that her house and all the petty
things that fill up most of her time belong to a greater
whole and take their place in the union of her people!'
Behind such a passage lie all the assumptions of
nationalist metaphysics and anthropology. It may serve
to distinguish nationalism from patriotism and
xenophobia with which it is often confused. Patriotism,
affection for one's country, or one's group, loyalty to its
institutions, and zeal for its defence, is a sentiment
known among all kinds of men; so is xenophobia,
which is dislike of the stranger, the outsider, and
reluctance to admit him into one's own group. Neither
sentiment depends on a particular anthropology and
neither asserts a particular doctrine of the state or of the
individual's relation to it. Nationalism does both; it is a
comprehensive doctrine which leads to a distinctive
style of politics. But far from being a universal
phenomenon, it is a product of European thought in the
last 150 years. If confusion exists, it is because
nationalist doctrine has annexed these universally held
sentiments to the service of a specific anthropology and
metaphysic. It is, therefore, loose and inexact to speak,
as is sometimes done, of British or American
nationalism when describing the thought of those who
recommend loyalty to British or American political
institutions. A British or an American nationalist would
have to define the British or the American nation in
terms of language, race, or religion, to require that all
those who conform to the definition should belong to
the British or American state, that all those who do not,
should cease so to belong, and to demand that all
British and American citizens should merge their will in
the will of the community. It is at once clear that

political thought of this kind is marginal and insignificant in Britain and America, and that those who speak of
British or American nationalism do not usually have
such views in mind.

Nationalism is also sometimes described as a new
tribalism. The analogy is meant to indicate that like the
tribe, the nation excludes and is intolerant of outsiders.
But such characteristics, as has been said, are common
to all human groups, and cannot serve to define either
tribe or nation. But the analogy is not only unable to
shed light on the matter, it can also mislead. A
tribesman's relation to his tribe is usually regulated in
minute detail by custom which is followed unquestion-
ingly and considered part of the natural or the divine
order. Tribal custom is neither a decree of the General
Will, nor an edict of legislative Reason. The tribesman
is such by virtue of his birth, not by virtue of self-
determination. He is usually unaware that the destiny of
man is progressive, and that he can fulfil this destiny by
merging his will into the will of the tribe. Nationalism
and tribalism, then, are not interchangeable terms, nor
do they describe related phenomena.

Another assertion often made is that nation-states
have been in the process of formation at least since the
sixteenth century; but this, again, seems a confusion,
which results from using nationalist categories in
historiography. When the peculiar anthropology and
metaphysics of nationalism are used in the interpretation of the past, history takes on quite another
complexion. Men who thought they were acting in
order to accomplish the will of God, to make the truth
prevail, or to advance the interests of a dynasty, or
perhaps simply to defend their own against aggression,
are suddenly seen to have been really acting in order
that the genius of a particular nationality should be
manifested and fostered. Abraham was not a man

possessed with the vision of the one God, he was really
the chieftain of a beduin tribe intent on endowing his
horde with a national identity. Moses was not a man
inspired by God in order to fulfil and re-affirm His
covenant with Israel, he was really a national leader
rising against colonial oppression. Muhammad may
have been the seal of the Prophets, but even more
important, he was the founder of the Arab nation.
Luther was a shining manifestation of Germanism; Hus
a precursor of Masaryk. Nationalists make use of the
past in order to subvert the present. One instance of this
transformation of the past occurs in a letter written
against Zionism by an orthodox rabbi of Eastern
Europe in 1900. In this letter, the Dzikover Rebbe
contrasts the traditional view which the community of
Israel had of itself, and the new nationalist interpretation of the Jewish past. Bitterness gives his speech a
biting concision, and this letter thus exhibits in a clear
and striking manner the operations of nationalist
historiography, as well as the traditional interpretation
which it has challenged. 'For our many sins,' writes the
Rebbe, 'strangers have risen to pasture the holy flock,
men who say that the people of Israel should be clothed
in secular nationalism, a nation like all other nations,
that Judaism rests on three things, national feeling, the
land and the language, and that national feeling is the
most praiseworthy element in the brew and the most
effective in preserving Judaism, while the observance of
the Torah and the commandments is a private matter
depending on the inclination of each individual. May
the Lord rebuke these evil men and may He who
chooseth Jerusalem seal their mouths.'[2] Nationalist
historiography operates, in fact, a subtle but unmistak-

---

[2] The Rebbe's letter is reproduced and translated in I. Domb,
The Transformation, 1958 (published by the author).

able change in traditional conceptions. In Zionism, Judaism ceases to be the *raison d'être* of the Jew, and becomes, instead, a product of Jewish national consciousness. In the doctrine of Pakistan, Islam is transformed into a political ideology and used in order to mobilize Muslims against Hindus; more than that it cannot do, since an Islamic state on classical lines is today an impossible anachronism. In the doctrine of the *Action Française* Catholicism becomes one of the attributes which define a true Frenchman and exclude a spurious one. This transformation of religion into nationalist ideology is all the more convenient in that nationalists can thereby utilize the powerful and tenacious loyalties which a faith held in common for centuries creates. These loyalties can be utilized even when they are not explicitly spoken of. There is little doubt that the appeal of modern Egyptian, or Panarab, or Armenian, or Greek nationalism derives the greater part of its strength from the existence of ancient communal and religious ties which have nothing to do with nationalist theory, and which may even be opposed to it. The Patriarch of Constantinople Gennadius (d.1468) may illustrate the traditional religious attitude towards ties of race and language: 'Though I am a Hellene by speech, yet I would never say that I was a Hellene', he wrote, 'for I do not believe as the Hellenes believed. I should like to take my name from my Faith, and if anyone asked me what I am answer "Christian".' But today, with the spread of nationalist doctrine, this opposition between Hellenism and orthodoxy is itself rejected. Orthodoxy and Hellenism are thought to go together and imply one another, as witnessed in the civil war of which Cyprus has been the stage.

Similarly, when nationalist historiography applies itself to the European past, it produces a picture of nations slowly emerging and asserting themselves in territorial sovereign states. It is, of course, undoubtedly the case that a number of territorial sovereignties succeeded in establishing themselves in Europe in modern times, and that gradually these sovereignties were strengthened and made durable by centralizing kings who were able to defeat particularisms and to establish everywhere the authority of their agents and of their 'state'. But these sovereignties were far from being 'nations', as the word is understood in nationalist parlance. The Habsburg Empire was a most powerful state, yet it was not a 'nation'; Prussia was the state at its most perfect, but it was not a 'nation'; Venice was a state which lasted for centuries: was it then a 'nation'? And such states have to be cited in illustration of the political development of modern Europe. Yet how easy is the confusion when, not these, but other European states are being considered; for it is but one step from talking about the French state under Philip the Fair, Henry the Fourth, and Louis the Fourteenth, to talking about the French 'nation' and its development under these monarchs. The continuity of the French state, or of the Spanish state, and their territorial stability, make it easy to adduce them as examples of the growth and development of European 'nations': the shift is vital, yet almost imperceptible. How vital it is may be appreciated when we remember that France is a state not because the French constitute a nation, but rather that the French state is the outcome of dynastic ambitions, of circumstances, of lucky wars, of administrative and diplomatic skills. It is these which maintained order, enforced laws, and carried out policies; these which made possible at last the cohesive existence of Frenchmen within the French state. It is such things which make possible the continuous existence of political communities, whether or not they are the 'nations' of nationalist theory. The matter becomes even clearer when nationalist historiography is made to deal, not with certain countries in modern Europe, where it has a kind of plausibility, but with countries in almost any other part of the world at almost any period of history. In the Roman Empire, the Ottoman Empire, Mogul India, pre-Conquest South America, or China the categories of nationalist historiography, taken seriously, must lead to a contorted, paradoxical, untenable picture of the past. What nationalist historiography professes to explain in the case of modern France or Spain or Italy or Germany, it must, in so many other cases, immediately hasten to explain away. The Ottoman Empire was not a 'nation', the Roman Empire was not a 'nation', and yet they were able, as few contemporary states have yet shown themselves able, to continue for centuries, to maintain the cohesion of the social fabric and to attract the loyalties of men. This confusion between states and 'nations' is facilitated by a particular feature of European political history, namely the existence of a European society of states in constant intercourse and conflict, who regulated their relations, however unwillingly and imperfectly, by a universally acknowledged *ius gentium*. Since nationalism sees the world as a world of many states, it seems but natural to consider a society of nations as the equivalent and continuation of the European society of states. But in reality the two are far removed. The European society of states knew a great diversity of governments and constitutions; a society of nations must be composed of nation-states, and any state which is not a nation-state has its title and its existence perpetually challenged. The national principle, then, far from providing continuity in European diplomacy, means a radical subversion of the European state system, an endless attempt to upset the balance of power on which the system must rest.

If nationalism cannot provide a satisfactory account of past political developments, neither can it supply a plain method whereby nations may be isolated from one another and constituted into sovereign states. The world is indeed diverse, much too diverse, for the classifications of nationalist anthropology. Races, languages, religions, political traditions and loyalties are so inextricably intermixed that there can be no clear convincing reason why people who speak the same language, but whose history and circumstances otherwise widely diverge, should form one state, or why people who speak two different languages and whom circumstances have thrown together should not form one state. On nationalist logic, the separate existence of Britain and America, and the union of English and French Canadians within the Canadian state, are both monstrosities of nature; and a consistent nationalist interpretation of history would reduce large parts of it to inexplicable and irritating anomalies. The inventors of the doctrine tried to prove that nations are obvious and natural divisions of the human race, by appealing to history, anthropology, and linguistics. But the attempt breaks down since, whatever ethnological or philological doctrine may be fashionable for the moment, there is no convincing reason why the fact that people speak the same language or belong to the same race should, by itself, entitle them to enjoy a government exclusively their own. For such a claim to be convincing, it must also be proved that similarity in one respect absolutely overrides differences in other respects. What remains in the doctrine is an affirmation that men have the right to stand on their differences from others, be these differences what they may, fancied or real, important or not, and to make of these differences their first political principle. Of course, academic disciplines, like philology, can make a powerful auxiliary for such a political doctrine, and enable it to secure conviction and assent, but they do not constitute the ultimate ground on which it takes its stand. Ernest Renan, in his lecture of 1882, *What is a Nation*, saw that this must be the case, and having examined the different criteria which are used to distinguish nations, and having found them wanting, concluded that the will of the individual must ultimately indicate whether a nation exists or not. Even if the existence of nations can be deduced from the principle of diversity, it still cannot be deduced what particular nations exist and what their precise limits are. What remains is to fall back on the will of the individual who, in pursuit of self-determination, wills himself as the member of a nation. The doctrine occasionally appears in its pure state, stripped of academic flannel and accidental accretions. The Jewish nationalist Ahad Ha'am (1856–1927) has a passage in which he discusses the fundamentals of Jewish nationality. It is a mistake, he writes, to think that Jewish nationality exists only when there is an actual collective national ethos. No doubt this national ethos came into being in consequence of a life lived in common over a number of generations. 'Once, however,' he argues, 'the spirit of nationality has so come into being . . . it becomes a phenomenon that concerns the individual alone, its reality being dependent on nothing but its presence in his psyche, and on no external or objective actuality. If I feel the spirit of Jewish nationality in my heart so that it stamps all my inward life with its seal, then the spirit of Jewish nationality exists in me; and its existence is not at an end even if all my Jewish contemporaries should cease to feel it in their hearts.' Here are no superfluous appeals to philology or biology, no laborious attempts to prove that because a group speaks the same language, or has the same religion, or lives in the same territory, it therefore is a nation. All this is casually brushed aside, and the nation, says Ahad Ha'am, is what individuals feel in their hearts is the nation. Renan's own description of the nation is that it is a daily plebiscite. The metaphor is felicitous, if only because it indicates so well that nationalism is ultimately based on will, and shows how inadequate the doctrine is in describing the political process, for a political community which conducts daily plebiscites must soon fall into querulous anarchy, or hypnotic obedience.

National self-determination is, in the final analysis, a determination of the will; and nationalism is, in the first place, a method of teaching the right determination of the will. This indeed is the fundamental subject of Fichte's *Addresses*. These lectures, we must note, were delivered in Berlin in the aftermath of the Prussian humiliation at Jena in 1806; they seek to explain why the Prussian state had been unable to withstand Napoleon, and to indicate what must be done to make good the disaster. Fichte had been an admirer of the French Revolution, at its most Jacobinical. What he valued most in the Revolution was the creation of a state where, as he thought, individual freedom would have meaning only in the collective being. Also, he and his contemporaries were impressed by the tremendous collective energy engendered by the Revolution. The revival of Prussia was possible only if the secret of the Revolution were penetrated, and used to generate some of that prodigious collective energy which had enabled the French to subjugate the whole of Europe. Administrative changes, a better organization of the armed forces, a more efficient bureaucracy, all these, Fichte was quite clear, would not answer. 'It is neither the strong right arm, nor the efficient weapon that wins victories, but only the power of the soul. . . . He who sets no limits whatever for himself, but, on the contrary, stakes everything he has, including the most precious possession granted to dwellers here below, namely, life itself, never ceases to resist, and will undoubtedly win the victory over an opponent whose goal is more limited.' Fichte's quest in the *Addresses* was for this wonderful power of the soul.

The *Moniteur de l'Empire*, the French official gazette, taking notice of the lectures as they were being delivered at the Royal Academy in Berlin, described them as 'public lectures given in Berlin by a celebrated German philosopher on the means for the improvement of education'. To the French censor, education must have seemed an innocuous subject, since he allowed the *Addresses* to be delivered and printed; but he ought to have known better, for had not his master, Napoleon, said: 'There will never be a fixed political state of things until we have a body of teachers instructed on established principles. So long as the people are not taught from their earliest years whether they ought to be republicans or royalists, Christians or infidels, the state cannot properly be called a nation.' For it was to education that Fichte looked to provide him with the key to the power of which he was in search. In his first address, he summed up his programme: 'In a word,' he said, 'it is a total change of the existing system of education that I propose as the sole means of preserving the existence of the German nation.' By this he did not mean that education ought properly to make the pupil familiar with and affectionate towards the traditions of his country, that German education, as it then existed, was not carrying out its duties. His meaning was somewhat different: 'What was lacking in the old system,' he noted, 'namely, an influence penetrating to the roots of vital impulse and action – the new education must supply.' 'By means of the new education', he added, 'we want to mould the Germans into a corporate body, which shall be stimulated and animated in all its individual members by the same interest.' If this could be done, then the nation as well as all its members would live in freedom. But how could it be done? Fichte's way was simple; simple because radical. 'The new education must consist essentially in this,' he reveals, 'that it completely destroys freedom of will in the soil which it undertakes to cultivate, and produces, on the contrary, strict necessity in the decisions of the will, the opposite being impossible.' A nation composed of such men is invincible; each of its members 'who has such a stable will, wills what he wills for ever, and cannot, under any circumstances, will otherwise than he always wills. For him freedom of the will is destroyed and swallowed up in necessity. . . . If you want to influence him at all, you must do more than merely talk to him; you must fashion him, and fashion him, and fashion him in such a way that he simply cannot will otherwise than you wish him to will.' 'The education proposed by me, therefore,' concludes Fichte, 'is a reliable and deliberate art for fashioning in man a stable and infallible good will.' This is why, on nationalist theory, education must have a central position in the work of the state. The purpose of education is not to transmit knowledge, traditional wisdom, and the ways devised by a society for attending to the common concerns; its purpose rather is wholly political, to bend the will of the young to the will of the nation. Schools are instruments of state policy, like the army, the police, and the exchequer. In his dialogue on *Patriotism and its Opposite*, Fichte says that a state which adopted his educational policy could dispense with an army, for then it 'would have a nation to put in arms, which simply could not be defeated by any mortal power'. The purpose of this education is to annex minds to love of the state, and therefore what is taught and how it is taught, what is suppressed and what is changed, is a matter of state policy. A personal recollection is here apposite. The incident happened in one of those ramshackle states of the Middle East set up after the First World War supposedly on the principle of national self-determination. A government of nationalists was determined to mould the extremely heterogeneous groups who were abandoned to its rule, willy-nilly, into one nation. One of the weapons it employed was to ensure that the teaching of what it pleased to call 'history' should be in the hands of its nominees, not only in its own establishments, but in private schools as well. The memory is still vivid of one such purveyor of 'history', an unemployed but eloquent lawyer, bursting out, his small dirty-green eyes blazing with passion, to exhort a class of astonished adolescents to remember that, in the national struggle, the gallows are a swing for heroes, exile a touristic holiday, and prison only a period of rest.[3] Politics embrace everything; the language men speak, the things they teach their children, the thoughts they revolve in their heads, love, marriage, maternity: the poet Leopardi is so overcome with nationalist fervour that, when his sister marries in 1821, he composes this *epithalamium*: 'O my sister, in these times of dejection, in these times of mourning, you will add one more unhappy family to unhappy Italy. Your sons will be either unhappy or cowards. Wish that they be unhappy!'

The total demand which nationalism makes on the individual originates, we must remember, in solicitude for his freedom. Real freedom, it holds, is a particular condition of the will which, once attained, ensures the lasting fulfilment of the individual and his bliss. Politics is a method of realizing this superhuman vision, of

---

[3] A variant of this saying is attributed to the well-known Muslim activist, Jamal al-Din al-Afghani (1838–97).

assuaging this metaphysical thirst. Such a politics is not concerned with reality. Its solitary object is an inner world and its end is the abolition of all politics; the realization of the real self in its real freedom is the annihilation of the actual self and of its imperfect freedom. The Romantics exhibit in their literature and often in their lives the violent, anarchic consequences of this metaphysical obsession; the romantic style indeed tends to blur and sometimes entirely obliterate the boundary between literature and life, between dreams and reality. The tragedy of Flaubert's Madame Bovary, it will be recalled, originated in her having read too many novels: Madame Bovary may stand not only as an archetype of romantic love, but also as a symbol of romantic politics, and nationalism may be described as a species of political bovarysme. One early Romantic writer who shows, both in his life and in his writings, the extreme signs of this metaphysical disorder is the German dramatist Heinrich von Kleist (1777–1811). His life seemed to alternate between bouts of listless melancholy and feverish activity; it was full of strange reticence and explosive violence; and he seemed possessed by some powerful, daemonic emotion, and to be engaged in an exasperated quest for some nameless ideal. He ended his short life by committing suicide in company with a young woman with whom he had had a short acquaintance. This explosive violence shows itself in some of his plays, notably *Hermann's Battle* (1808), the political theme of which is doubly significant. The play forcibly illustrates, in the first place, the nationalist view of political ends and means, and is, in the second place, strangely prophetic of the insatiable appetite the Nazis were later to show for purposeless and monstrous atrocities. The play was written under the impact of Prussia's and Austria's humiliation at the hand of Napoleon, and it uses the theme of Hermann's struggle against the Roman legions for exciting hatred of the French. In order to rally the Germanic tribes against the Romans, this chieftain sends his men disguised as Romans with the mission of burning and looting German villages; on his instructions, a virgin whom a Roman had raped, and whom her father had killed in order to escape dishonour, is divided into fifteen portions and sent to the fifteen Germanic tribes; when Hermann is told of the kindly deed of a Roman who had saved a German child from the flames, he exclaims: 'May he be cursed if he has done this! He has made for a moment my heart disloyal, he made me betray for a moment the august cause of Germany.' He shows his disappointment when he is informed that the Roman troops are well behaved: 'But I was counting, by all the Gods of revenge,' he bursts out, 'on fire, loot, violence, murder, and on all the horrors of unbridled war! What need have I of Latins who use me well?' It is not Hermann, however, but his wife Thusnelda who provides the emotional climax of the play. She is offended by the behaviour of the Roman Legate, whom she had thought to be in love with her, and whom she then discovers to be insincere. Tempting him with an amorous meeting, she entices him into an enclosed garden, where he finds himself face to face with a savage and famished she-bear. Thusnelda stands outside, watching the terrified Legate and advising him to make love to this other Thusnelda who is in the garden with him; and as the beast pounces on the Legate, Thusnelda falls into a swoon with the intensity of pleasurable horror. It is at these extremes of human nature which they knew so well how to explore, where horror and delight, love and hate, cruelty and tenderness are indistinguishable, that the Romantics sought a heightened, transformed, superhuman existence, which might abolish life as it is actually lived;

nationalism is the political expression of this quest. The historian Meinecke relates that General Beck once in the nineteen-thirties remarked to him of Hitler: 'This fellow has no Fatherland at all.'[4] The remark is just and serves to make clear the difference between ordinary politics, which is concerned to maintain the state of the world and to provide for the safety and prosperity of an actual state and actual citizens, and the nihilist frenzy of Nazism.

Nationalism looks inwardly, away from and beyond the imperfect world. And this contempt of things as they are, of the world as it is, ultimately becomes a rejection of life, and a love of death. The obsession of the Romantics with death is well known. Schleiermacher writes of death with lyric fervour: '. . . may it be the mission of my freedom,' he exclaims in the *Soliloquies*, 'to bring me nearer to this necessity. May it be my highest goal to be able to wish to die!' Life is imperfection constantly struggling for the perfection of death. It must be lived to the utmost, and the struggle go on unremittingly, until, finally, the vigour of youth yields at once to the perfection of death. Old age is an abatement of the struggle, a failure of the will; it is a confession of defeat by time, by the biological process, by dull, inert matter; it is a mistake which must and can be avoided: 'The decline of vigour and of strength,' observed Schleiermacher, 'is an ill that man inflicts upon himself; old age is but an idle prejudice, an ugly fruit of the mad delusion that the spirit is dependent on the body.' It is wrong to imagine that wisdom and age go together. Wisdom is acquired through experience, and always to be acquiring experience needs eternal youth: 'What I aspire to know and make my own is infinite, and only in an infinite series of attempts', asserts

---

4 F. Meinecke, *The German Catastrophe*, 1950.

Schleiermacher, 'can I completely fashion my own being. The spirit that drives man forward, and the constant appeal of new goals, that can never be satisfied by past achievements, shall never depart from me.' We see here a departure, pregnant with consequences, from a very old and almost universal belief, namely, that while impetuosity is the apanage of youth, wisdom is the hallmark of age, and that youth must not be entrusted with power.

> Age is deformèd, youth unkind;

notes the poet,

> We scorn their bodies, they our mind.

But if life is imperfection constantly struggling for the ultimate perfection of death, then age becomes not merely deformed, but foolish. To be eternally young, as the term goes, becomes desirable and praiseworthy. Politics, in particular, becomes eminently the province of the young. For politics is not the conciliation of interests, not the safeguard of social institutions; had it been only these, then old men, whom passions have ceased to tempt, whose resolution is cold and deliberate, might be preferred to youth. But since politics is an infinite quest, a ceaseless striving, gerontocracy must be rejected, and paedocracy instituted. This emphasis on youth and death explains the frequent violence and horror of nationalist methods: politics is a passionate assertion of the will, but at the core of this passion is a void, and all its activity is the frenzy of despair; it is a search for the unattainable which, once attained, destroys and annihilates. The perceptive Heine looked at these new dogmas and understood where things were tending: 'There will be', he said in *Religion and*

Philosophy in Germany (1834), 'Kantians forthcoming who in the new world to come will know nothing of reverence for aught, and who will ravage without mercy, and riot with sword and axe through the soil of all European life to dig out the last root of the past; there will be well-weaponed Fichteans on the ground, who in the fanaticism of the Will, are not to be restrained by fear or self-advantage, for they live in the Spirit.'

It is, then, a misunderstanding to ask whether nationalism is politics of the right or of the left. It is neither. Left and right are concepts which arose in the course of struggle between aristocracy, middle class and working class in European countries in the nineteenth and twentieth centuries, and are unintelligible apart from this particular history. In the nineteenth century, it was usual to consider nationalism a progressive, democratic, leftist movement. The nationalists of 1848 were considered men of the left; Mazzini was a highly venerated figure among English Liberals and Radicals, as was Kossuth, the Hungarian nationalist; to support nationalist movements in Europe and elsewhere was considered the duty of every true Liberal and humanitarian. This conjunction is, as will be seen, a fortuitous accident, but the habits of mind it established have lasted into the twentieth century, when Liberals and Socialists think that their principles require them to support nationalist movements, particularly in Asia and Africa. But it is also significant that nationalists who, at one stage, were considered men of the left were, at a later stage, firmly denounced as men of the right: Pilsudski, Mussolini, Chiang Kai-shek, all began their careers as men of the left, and all, in time, were removed to the right. Hitler, it may be added, could also be considered as a man of the left, for he was the leader of a *National Socialist German Workers' Party*, yet he is now firmly and universally classified as a man of the right. These confusions are significant. What they indicate is that the categories of one ideology are used to test and classify the tenets of a completely different ideology. Liberals measure political progress by the diminution of social and political privileges, and for Socialists the touchstone of progress is the reduction of economic inequality. To nationalists, such aims are incidental and secondary. Their own aim is national self-determination, and the lasting fulfilment which comes to man when he lives as a member of a sovereign nation.

But this confusion, whether nationalism is a right-wing or a left-wing movement, has become greatly prevalent owing to the triumph of Bolshevism in Russia, and the wide popularity and respect which the writings of its leaders, Lenin and Stalin, have attained. Now the attitude of the Bolshevik leaders towards national problems was a strict and subordinate corollary of their Marxism, and of the struggle for revolutionary social-ism which engaged all their energies. In their theory, national movements could be both progressive and retrogressive, depending on the stage of economic development at which they occurred. In their progres-sive phase, they were an expression of the struggle of bourgeois capitalism against social and political domination which had outlived its economic justifica-tion. Nationalism was a progressive movement so long as the capitalist struggle against feudalism had not been won; it was a progressive movement in the colonial and semi-colonial world, when it embodied the struggle of a national bourgeoisie against imperialism – itself, in the title of Lenin's pamphlet of 1916, the highest stage of capitalism. But nationalism became retrogressive when it threw up obstacles to the advance of socialism, when it was the ideology of bankrupt capitalist expropriators, unjustly resisting their own expropriation. Again, in their polemical writings which sometimes approved, and sometimes disapproved, of nationalist movements in Tsarist Russia, Lenin's and Stalin's criterion was whether such movements advanced or retarded the cause of revolution. Thus, Lenin was opposed to the claims of the Jewish working-class party, the Bund, for Jewish autonomy in Eastern Europe, because such a claim weakened and divided the leadership of the socialist movement; but he also criticized the socialist Rosa Luxemburg for neglecting and belittling Polish nationalism, as a weapon with which to undermine the Tsarist autocracy. Such a line of reasoning makes it easy to understand why to Bolsheviks nationalism is a right-wing movement in contemporary Europe, and a left-wing movement in Asia and Africa. But it ought also to become clear that the wide acceptance of such classifications depends on a tacit, uncritical acquiescence in the Marxist interpretation of history.

6

NATIONALISM AND
POLITICS: I

A T THE time when the doctrine was being elaborated,
Europe was in turmoil. The Revolution had
succeeded in destroying the Monarchy and the traditional social order in France. Not only its example and
influence, but its actions and policies carried the
disturbance outwards from France in ever-widening
ripples. 'By sending us as deputies here,' Danton said in
the Convention of 1792, 'the French nation has brought
into being a grand committee for the general insurrection of the peoples.' Napoleon, who followed, completed the destructive action of the Revolution. In a short
career, of less than twenty years, he laid low the fabric
of international order in Europe. Things which had not
been thought possible were now seen to be indeed
possible and feasible. Revolutions could succeed,
empires be overthrown, and frontiers changed. A man,
a handful of men, by resolution, audacity, and ruthless-
ness could raise masses of other men to decide the fate
of governments and the frontiers of states. So much
turbulence and so much violence from 1789 to 1815
could not fail to have far-reaching consequences. It
revived old enmities and created new ones; classes of
society which had never dreamt of exercising power
tasted of it by proxy, and would never again relapse into
obedient tameness; hopes were kindled, passions
aroused which were impossible to extinguish. The

Congress of Vienna tried to restore the European system
disrupted by the Revolution and by Napoleon; the great
Powers, the position of which the Congress recognized
and consecrated, were England, Prussia, Austria, Russia,
and France, the same states, that is, whose interlocking
policies had made possible a balance of power before
1789. It was now thought that the system could again
be set up, and the dance resumed where it had been so
rudely disturbed.

But, of course, the dance could not be resumed, at
least not to the same tune. Too much had happened in
the meantime, and too much was still happening. Not
only could the Revolution not be unmade, but Revolution as a possible kind of political action would
henceforth always be present in the European consciousness as a promise and a threat. Alfred de Musset, who
mirrors in his work the unease and the latent violence of
the generation which grew to maturity in the aftermath
of the Napoleonic era, expressed the matter well when
he said in his *Confession d'un Enfant du Siècle* (1836)
that Napoleon parodied kingship and destroyed it. In
the past, de Musset wrote, it happened that individual
kings showed that countenance of terror which incited
the people to fall on them and tear them like savage
dogs; but it was only during the Revolution and the
Empire, he observed, that all the pillars of society,
without exception, the kings, the nobles, the Church,
manifested all at the same time that loss of nerve, those
fatal signs of fear which irrevocably lost them
everything. Napoleon had come and gone; the
victorious Powers tried to ensure that he would never
return, and to undo all that he did, but the kind of
policy Napoleon pursued was a standing example to
anybody who had ambition and ability to imitate him,
and Napoleonic traditions would always have an
appeal to those sections of European society which his

opportunism had, at different times, led him to court and favour. One feature, in particular, of Napoleonic policies is highly pertinent to the later spread of nationalism. While still a general, serving under the Directory, in 1796–7, Bonaparte invaded Italy and occupied Venice; the better to tame the Venetian Senate, he sent emissaries to the Ionian Islands, then under Venetian rule, among them a 'distinguished man of letters' whose duty was to 'manufacture manifestoes' in order 'to stir up the shades of Sparta and Athens', to raise up the inhabitants against their masters by reminding them of the ancient glories of Greece, and exhorting them to resuscitate these glories. As Emperor, Napoleon continued the same tactics. Quarrelling with the Habsburg Emperor in 1809, he issued a proclamation to the Hungarians saying: 'You have national customs and a national language; you boast of a distant and illustrious origin: take up then once again your existence as a nation. Have a king of your choice, who will rule only for you, who will live in the midst of you, whom only your citizens and your soldiers will serve. . . . Meet therefore in a National Diet, in the manner of your ancestors . . . and let me know your decisions.' When he decided to invade Russia he enlisted the aid of the Poles in his enterprise, by promising to restore the Polish state, and by actually setting up the Grand Duchy of Warsaw. 'Show yourselves worthy of your forefathers,' he said to a Polish deputation, 'they ruled the House of Brandenburg, they were the masters of Moscow, they took the fortress of Widdin, they freed Christianity from the yoke of the Turks.' He set up the Kingdom of Italy, and his coadjutor Murat, whom he made King of Naples, at the last minute, to escape the retribution of the Allies in 1815, attempted to gain Italian support against Austrian arms by proclaiming the unity and independence of Italy. The Austrian commander in Italy might exhort the Italian to pay no heed to these chimeras: 'What makes a people happy?' he asked. 'It is not to form an extensive and populous nation. It is good laws, the preservation of ancient traditions, and a thrifty administration.' But even though Napoleon was defeated, and the old masters reinstated, the hopes of political power which he had aroused in so many would not be forgotten; should favouring circumstances ever arise, the hopes could again be fanned into a flame.

This was one reason why, in spite of the efforts of the victorious Powers, Europe in 1815 could not take up once again the way of life interrupted in 1789. There were others. At the same time as this upheaval was taking place in the political habits of the continent, its social structure was being radically transformed. The Industrial Revolution, accompanied by a prodigious increase in population, was gradually penetrating everywhere, transforming methods of production, disturbing traditional social relations and creating vast urban agglomerations. New wealth was being created and new social classes were coming to the top who would, sooner or later, claim and obtain their share of political power. To the new classes politics presented themselves in a guise different from that familiar to the absolute monarchs and the nobility in whose hands lay the destiny of Europe in the eighteenth century. To these, the countries they ruled were a personal and family concern; their family relations and combinations extended all over Europe regardless of linguistic and religious differences, or of international frontiers, and they were as powerful a factor as any in deciding the fate of a country or a province. In contrast to them, the new social classes had no such ties to claim their attention and loyalty. That German-speaking lands should be parcelled out among a multitude of kings, princes, and other lesser sovereignties may have seemed natural to some of the negotiators at Vienna in 1815; the claims they were accustomed to deal with were dynastic and familial, reinforced or weakened by military preponderance or inferiority; once, therefore, the Napoleonic structure was demolished, they found it reasonable to revert to the earlier systems. But what had seemed before 1789 an established order of things, began increasingly to look an absurd anachronism. If Napoleon was able to arrange and rearrange at will the map of Europe, then no ancient prescription, no dynastic tie, had any claim to stand in the way of more rational and natural arrangements.

Europe after 1815 then was destined to a long period of unrest. The victors did their best to ensure that the settlement they devised would be lasting, but the turmoil bequeathed from revolutionary and Napoleonic times, and the inexorable social changes, acting separately or jointly, always threatened, and in the end overthrew the 1815 settlement. Those who opposed it did so on the ground that it took no account of the wishes of the peoples, that rulers were imposed on subjects who had not been consulted, and that territories which were naturally one were artificially separated. The two grievances were entwined with each other, both of them indeed the outcome of philosophical speculations which had preceded and accompanied the French Revolution. Of course this is not to say that every nationalist and every libertarian in revolt against the arrangements of the Congress of Vienna was competent to explain on what metaphysical grounds he believed that men had the right to decide who was to govern them, and that humanity was divided, naturally, into nations. These ideas became the commonplaces of radicalism on the continent, and young men, university students, in Italy, Germany, and Central Europe found it reasonable to believe in these things, and heroic to be enrolled in a secret society dedicated to Liberty and Nationality. Joseph Mazzini (1805–72), son of a worthy Genoese family, destined by his parents to a respectable professional career, came, in the 1820s, while still a student, to be enrolled in the secret society of the Carbonari, to dabble in conspiracy, and handle subversive prints, to carry out secret missions on the orders of persons quite unknown to him, and as to whose real aims he was completely ignorant, eventually to be picked up by the police, and sent to gaol in a fortress, thereafter to spend a lifetime of poverty and exile, always engaged in feeble conspiracy and wordy exhortation. 'At the moment when the Sbiri seized me,' he tells us in his autobiography, 'I had matter enough for three condemnations upon me: rifle-bullets; a letter in cipher . . .; a history of the three days of July, printed on tricoloured paper, the formula of the oath for the *second rank* of Carbonari; and, moreover (for I was arrested in the act of leaving the house) a sword-stick. I succeeded in getting rid of everything. They had all the inclination, but not sufficient capacity for tyranny. The long perquisitions made in our house led to no dangerous discovery.' Why should a young man of respectable family, in comfortable circumstances, encumber himself with these ridiculous properties, and expose himself to the unwelcome attentions of authority? He was living under a government which, as governments go, was not really intolerable: it did not levy ruinous taxation, it did not conscript soldiers, it did not maintain concentration camps, and it left its subjects pretty much to their own devices. It was perhaps somewhat obscurantist and cumbersome but, as Mazzini himself says, it had not sufficient capacity for tyranny. It is not here that we must seek for an explanation of young Mazzini's behaviour. It is rather

to be found in Mazzini himself, in a spiritual restlessness which he shared with his generation, which made
him and his fellows dissatisfied with things as they were,
and prodigiously eager for change. The generation
which was born during the Empire, de Musset said, was
'passionate, pale, restless'. They had been nurtured in
constant commotion, and lived in daily expectation of
change, eager for new excitements, and sceptical of
stability and rest. 'Three elements,' he wrote, 'constituted life as it offered itself then to the young men:
behind them a past destroyed for ever, but still restless
and agitated over its own ruins, with all the fossils of
the centuries of absolutism; in front of them the dawn
of an immense horizon, the first daybreak of the future;
and between these two worlds . . . something similar to
the Ocean which divides the old world from young
America, something, I know not what, vague and
indeterminate, a stormy sea full of shipwreck.'

The restlessness of this generation surrounded those
legendary times of the Revolution and the Empire with
a haze of glory, and the political methods which they
introduced had now the glamour and headiness of the
forbidden. Extra-legal action became infinitely seduct-
ive, and conspiracies, riots, infernal machines were
invested with an efficacy for which doctrine, not
experience, provided the warrant. 'Insurrection,' say the
Instructions for the members of Young Italy, the secret
society which Mazzini founded in 1831, '– by means of
guerilla bands – is the true method of warfare for all
nations desirous of emancipating themselves from a
foreign yoke. . . . It forms the military education of the
people, and consecrates every foot of the native soil by
the memory of some warlike deed.' 'Guerilla warfare,'
we read in the *Rules for the Conduct of Guerilla Bands*,
which he composed, 'opens a field of activity for every
local capacity; forces the enemy into an unaccustomed

method of battle; avoids the evil consequences of a great defeat; secures the national war from the risk of treason, and has the advantage of not confining it within any defined and determinate basis of operations. It is invincible, indestructible.' This is a rousing and a heady doctrine, but neither then nor later did it lead to success. Conspiracies and agitations by students and ex-students led to nothing much. Italian independence was achieved by the persistent ambition of the House of Savoy and the muddled policies of Napoleon III who thought it worth while to go to war with Austria on its behalf; German unity was the work of Bismarck, who was not a nationalist, but a promoter of Prussian interests; Balkan nationalisms could show results only because they were adopted by the Russian State which sought thereby to encroach on the Ottoman domain; Arab nationalism has found resonance and extension as a result of British policies which sought to prosecute a long-standing rivalry with France, and to eliminate the influence of other great Powers from the Middle East; and it was Japan's help and encouragement which enabled Indonesian and Burmese nationalists to set up a political and military organization whereby to wrest control, in the chaos following the Second World War, from the old imperial Powers. Where nationalists found no Power effectively to espouse their cause their conspiracies and insurrections very often came to nought. This is what happened to the Hungarians in 1848, to the Poles in their risings in 1831, 1846, and 1863, and to the Armenians of the Ottoman Empire at the end of the nineteenth century.

But the restlessness was the work not only of the revolutionary legend; it proceeded from a breakdown in the transmission of political habits and religious beliefs from one generation to the next. In societies suddenly exposed to the new learning and the new philosophies of the Enlightenment and of Romanticism, orthodox settled ways began to seem ridiculous and useless. The attack was powerful and left the old generation bewildered and speechless; or if it attempted to speak, it merely gave voice to irritated admonition, obstinate opposition, or horror-stricken rejection, which only served to widen the rift and increase the distance between the fathers and the sons. There is a pathetic poem by the Russian-Jewish writer, J. L. Gordon (1830–92), which expresses this very alienation of the young intellectual from his environment, and his feeling of total incomprehension. 'The muse still furtively visits me; my heart stilt yearns, and my hand writes; it still writes poems in a language forgotten. What salvation is there for me? What craving left? What goal? For whom have I toiled all my best years, denying myself contentment and peace? . . . My parents, clinging to their God and their people, are busy with trading all day and observing commandments; true knowledge they spurn, good taste they have never acquired. "Death is in poetry; heresy in noble expression", so they scold us and wrathfully rant.' The sons rejected the fathers and their ways; but the rejection extended also to the very practices, traditions, and beliefs which had over the centuries moulded and fashioned these societies which suddenly seemed to the young so confining, so graceless, so devoid of spiritual comfort, and so unable to minister to the dignity and fulfilment of the individual. Thus, in another poem Gordon bitterly attacks Rabbinical Judaism which, after the Dispersion, by means of teaching, prescription, and the continuous leadership of its learned men, kept together the community of Israel, and impressed it with a distinctive character. 'They have destroyed thee, O Israel,' exclaims Gordon against the Rabbis, 'for they have not taught thee to wage war with skill and knowledge. . . . For centuries thy teachers have directed thee, building houses of study: and what have they taught thee? They have taught thee to tend the wind, to plough the stone, to draw water in a sieve, to thresh straw. They have taught thee, alas, to go against life, to shut thyself up alone within fences and walls, to be dead on earth and alive in heaven, to dream awake and speak in visions. And so thy sap is gone, thy spirit is enfeebled, thy heart is troubled, thy strength is dried up. They have battened thee with the dust of scribes and musty tomes, and have set thee before the world like a living mummy.' This violent revolt against immemorial restraints, this strident denunciation of decorum and measure, was inevitably accompanied by powerful social strains which may explain the dynamic and violent character of nationalist movements. These movements are ostensibly directed against the foreigner, the outsider, but they are also the manifestation of a species of civil strife between the generations; nationalist movements are children's crusades; their very names are manifestoes against old age: Young Italy, Young Egypt, the Young Turks, the Young Arab Party. When they are stripped of their metaphysics and their slogans – and these cannot adequately account for the frenzy they conjure up in their followers – such movements are seen to satisfy a need, to fulfil a want. Put at its simplest, the need is to belong together in a coherent and stable community. Such a need is normally satisfied by the family, the neighbourhood, the religious community. In the last century and a half such institutions all over the world have had to bear the brunt of violent social and intellectual change, and it is no accident that nationalism was at its most intense where and when such institutions had little resilience and were ill-prepared to withstand the powerful attacks to which they became exposed. This seems a more satisfactory account than to say that nationalism is a middle-class movement. It is the case that the German inventors of nationalist doctrine came from a class which could be called the middle class, and that they were discontented with the old order in which the nobility was predomin-ant. But the term middle class is closely tied to a particular area and a particular history, that of Western Europe. It presupposes and implies a distinct social order of which feudalism, municipal franchises, and rapid industrial development are some of the prominent features. Such features are not found in all societies, and it would therefore be misleading to link the existence of a nationalist movement to that of a middle class. In countries of the Middle and the Far East, for instance, where the significant division in society was between those who belonged to the state institution and those who did not, nationalism cannot be associated with the existence of a middle class. It developed, rather, among young officers and bureaucrats, whose families were sometimes obscure, sometimes eminent, who were educated in Western methods and ideas, often at the expense of the State, and who as a result came to despise their elders, and to hanker for the shining purity of a new order to sweep away the hypocrisy, the corruption, the decadence which they felt inexorably choking them and their society.

This breakdown in the transmission of political experience explains why nationalist movements run to extremes. Political wisdom is not to be gathered in the drab, arid world in which we actually live, it is to be culled from books of philosophy. A sober administrator might ask what philosophy had to do with rule. 'Sully, Colbert, Pitt, Bernstorff, Campomanes and Pombal,' observed Kampenhausen, a Russian civil servant early in the nineteenth century, 'were not worse administra-tors than we, even though they did not have the benefit of learning [philosophy] at the university.' But this, in the sight of passionate young men, was worldly wisdom, of the kind which leads to perdition. Literature and philosophy gave entrance to a nobler, truer world, a world more real and more exciting than the actual world; and gradually the boundary between the world of imagination and the world of reality became blurred, and sometimes disappeared altogether. What was possible in books ought to be possible in reality. The reading of books became a political, a revolutionary, activity. Thus, many a young man found himself advancing from the composition of poems to the manufacture of infernal machines; thus, in the intoxication of a poetic dream, Adam Mickiewicz found himself imploring God to bring about universal war in which Poland might once again secure independence. Politics could indeed be exciting, as exciting as the wonderful speculations of Schelling and Fichte. Mean provincial towns where nothing ever happens, dusty libraries, prosaic lecture-rooms became the stage of an absorbing secret game, a game of hide-and-seek, in which nothing was as it seemed, and everything took on the glowing colours of romance. Such are the delights of conspiracy. Occasionally. of course, the drabness would break in, and there would be policemen, arrests, prison, or exile. The enclosed, secret universe of plot and conspiracy would begin to exercise an obsessive compulsion of its own, from which escape was hopeless; what started as a poetic dream would be enacted with inexorable logic as a living nightmare, in which pistols did really go off, and dynamite did really explode; where men were caught up in a web of suspicion and treason, and today's executioner became tomorrow's victim. Consider the case of the schoolboys of Plovdiv who, in 1896, formed a Macedonian terrorist group. They began by stealing their parents' jewellery; one of them then committed suicide because he could raise no more money; others stole three hundred pounds from a post office with a forged cheque, and kidnapped two fellow-conspirators, who persuaded their parents to ransom them. Or again, consider the case of Mara Buneva who was happily married to a Bulgarian officer. In 1927, on the orders of the Internal Macedonian Revolutionary Organization, she went to Yugoslavia and opened a hat shop at Skolpje and made friends with a lawyer who had incurred the enmity of IMRO. 'At midday on January 13, 1928, Mara closed her shop. She went to the bridge over the Vardar where she would meet Prelitch on his way to lunch. She stopped him, then pulled a revolver from her blouse and fired. Prelitch fell mortally wounded. Then Mara shot herself. "I am sorry I had to kill Prelitch", said the poor girl before she died, "because he helped me several times." '[1] How and at what point, we wonder, did the schoolboys abandon their schoolboyish avocations, and the housewife forsake her housewifely cares, and became ready to commit crime and bloodshed?

'Human speech,' thundered Magnitski, rector of Kazan University in 1817, 'this it is, which transmits this diabolical power; the printing press is its weapon. University professors distil into the minds of unhappy youth the atrocious poison of unbelief and hatred of legitimate authorities.' The violence of this language may incline the reader to dismiss as mere obscurantism what is, in fact, a shrewd appreciation of the ultimate incompatibility of philosophical speculation with the civil order. This incompatibility rarely became apparent when philosophers were men of discretion teaching orally a small circle of disciples; when, however, it became really possible to print and disseminate books cheaply and speedily, and introduce them to all sorts and conditions of men, the problem, in some societies

[1] J. Swire, *Bulgarian Conspiracy*, 1939.

perhaps more than in others, was bound to become crucial. Magnitski, of course, errs when he implies that the whole process was a conscious, diabolical conspiracy. It was much more serious, for conspiracies can be discovered and broken, while the logic of a situation which nobody has designed or desired sometimes imposes a mastery against which it is vain to struggle. 'When asked by my father of what I was accused,' says Mazzini, recounting the story of his early arrest and imprisonment, '[the Governor of Genoa] replied that the time had not yet arrived for answering that question, but that I was a young man of talent, very fond of solitary walks by night, and habitually silent as to the subject of my meditations, *and that the government was not fond of young men of talent, the subject of whose musings was unknown to it.*' There was no efficacious means of controlling the musings of such young men, for they were not the fruit of a conspiracy. They were inherent in the nature of things; they emanated from the very spirit of the age.

The musings of the young men dwelt on two grievances: that governments were not popular, and that they were not national. It could, of course, be reasonably argued that governments were not popular because they were not national, that because governments were controlled by foreigners, they could not minister to the welfare of the ruled. The converse of this could also be argued, namely, that once governments became national, they would come under the control of the citizens and become agencies for their welfare. This notion that national government meant popular government was made plausible by the settlement of 1815. The victorious Powers not only restored dynasties to their thrones, ignoring 'national' boundaries and 'national' units, as these came to be understood by European radicals, but they also declared their enmity to the principles proclaimed by the Revolution. They proscribed representative institutions and restored privileges abolished by the Revolutionaries. It was thought to follow therefore that if the 1815 settlement were overthrown, then not only would nations assume their natural sovereign rights, but also that democratic ideas would triumph, and that these sovereign nations would practise Liberty, Equality, and Fraternity. War would then disappear, for all these nations would be, *ipso facto*, pacific and just. These commonplaces of nationalist thinking in the first half of the nineteenth century can be followed in Mazzini's writings. A nation, he writes, 'is a larger or smaller aggregate of human beings bound together into an organic whole by agreement in a certain number of real particulars, such as race, physiognomy, historic tradition, intellectual peculiarities, or active tendencies.' Nations, Mazzini believed, exist according to a divine design which evil governments have disfigured. 'They have disfigured it,' he says, 'by their conquests, their greed, and their jealousy even of the righteous power of others.' 'We are not only conspirators,' he writes in a note on the organization of Young Italy, the secret society he founded, 'but believers. We aspire to be not only revolutionists; but so far as we may, regenerators.' 'The peoples,' he also wrote, 'will only reach the highest point of development of which they are capable when they are united in a single bond. . . . Young Italy recognizes therefore the universal association of the peoples as the ultimate aim of the endeavours of all free men. . . . Before they can become members of the great association,' however, 'it is necessary that they should have a separate existence, name and power. Every people is therefore bound to constitute itself a nation before it can occupy itself with the question of humanity.'

But of course it was not, it could not be, as simple as that, if only because of another commonplace nationalist attitude: 'Avoid compromises,' lays down Mazzini, 'they are almost always immoral as well as dangerous.' For if there is a divine plan which divides humanity into nations, which evil governments have disfigured, there must be no truck with evil. The relation between a country and its foreign ruler must always take the shape of a 'desperate struggle'. 'Desperate struggle' is not kind to political liberties, and a hatred of compromise can easily turn into a hatred of those who may be suspected of compromise. It is a well-known feature of recent history that nationalist parties kill members of their own nationality whom they suspect of an inclination to compromise, and in some cases a greater number of these than of the foreigners against whom the struggle is waged fall to the assassin's bullet. A remarkable document may be cited here. In 1893 the Armenian nationalists who were trying to gain Armenian independence by violence posted this notice in Sivas: 'Osmanlis! . . . the examples are before your eyes. How many hundreds of rascals in Constantinople, Van, Erzeroum, Alashkert, Harpout, Cesarea, Marsovan, Asmassia and other towns have been killed by the Armenian revolutionists? What were these rascals? Armenians! Armenians! and again Armenians! If our aim was against the Mohammedans or Mohammedanism, as the Government tries to make you think, why should we kill the Armenians?' If only because of this, nationalism and political liberties may be extremely difficult to reconcile. In any case national government and constitutional government do not necessarily go together. Greece and the Balkan states succeeded in wresting national independence from the Ottoman Empire. The grievances of the subject areas were national grievances; they were ruled by a government alien in language and religion. But their chequered history since independence suggests that national freedom is no guarantee against oppressive and iniquitous government. New ruling classes replaced the evicted Ottomans, and found extreme difficulty in ruling humanely and effectively. Neither did the formation of these national states conduce, as Mazzini hoped, to international peace. It may, of course, be argued, as the poet Wordsworth argued, that native oppression is preferable to foreign oppression. 'The difference between inbred oppression and that which is from without is essential,' he observed in *The Convention of Cintra* (1809), 'inasmuch as the former does not exclude from the minds of the people a feeling of being self- governed; does not imply (as the latter does, when patiently submitted to) an abandonment of the first duty imposed by the faculty of reason.' The argument is plainly sophistical, but it does recognize, by implication, as Mazzini's does not, the truth established by experience, namely, that the triumph of the national principle does not necessarily entail the triumph of liberty.

A variant of Mazzini's argument has found great vogue in recent decades in Asiatic and African countries. This variant depends on an economic interpretation of history. It is to the effect that European Powers in search of markets and cheap raw materials have imposed their direct domination or indirect influence on these areas overseas and have thus distorted their political development, stunted their economies and insulted the human dignity of their inhabitants. It is also widely argued that the liberation of these countries from European rule makes possible the creation of free societies which would bring fulfilment and contentment to their citizens. But the economic foundation on which this theory rests serves to make the domination of Europe overseas seem both tentacular and intangible. For the domination, it is argued, does not always rest on naked force: the sinister power of money holds in its grip countries outwardly independent, and rulers seemingly patriotic; and full independence with all its blessings will only come when indirect as well as direct domination will have disappeared. This variant exhibits with particular clarity the fallacy of associating national independence with efficient, humane, and just government. It is manifestly not European domination which created poverty, technical backwardness, over-population, or habits of despotism in Asia and Africa – it is these rather which made possible European rule overseas; and it is not the departure of European rulers – after so brief a dominion – which will change the nature of these territories, transform their poverty into wealth, or suddenly create probity in judges, moderation and public spirit in statesmen, or honesty in public servants. The truth is that good government depends as much on circumstances as on a desire for freedom and there are regions of the globe which may never know its blessings. But it is characteristic of doctrines such as self-determination to disregard the limits imposed by nature and history, and to believe that a good will alone can accomplish miracles.

In fact, it is these countries which most clearly show that nationalism and liberalism far from being twins are really antagonistic principles. In these countries, constitutionalism is unknown. Their political tradition is either a centralized despotism, which, as a method of government, has shown itself extraordinarily resilient and durable, or a fragmented tribalism which has withered and fossilized as it has come in contact with European rule. In the first case, the central mechanism of power is all-important, since to get hold of it is to acquire mastery over the whole of society. Machiavelli remarked in *The Prince* that a conqueror might easily gain possession of a country like France, but find it very troublesome to keep, since it contained many divergent interests and sectional loyalties, not easily reconciled or subdued. A state like the Ottoman Empire, on the other hand, would be most difficult to conquer, but once conquered the subjects would be submissive and quite easy to govern: 'The Turkish Empire,' as he says, 'is governed by a sole Prince, all others being his slaves. Dividing his kingdom into sandjaks, he sends thither different governors whom he shifts and changes at his pleasure. The King of France, on the other hand, is surrounded by a multitude of nobles of ancient descent, each acknowledged and loved by subjects of his own, and each asserting a precedence in rank of which the King can deprive him only at his peril.' Once, therefore, the Sultan's army is defeated 'no cause of anxiety would remain, except in the family of the Prince, which being extirpated, there would be none else to fear'. The same explanation holds for the success and frequency of *coups d'état* in despotisms, as well as for the phenomenal spread of nationalism in them in modern times.

In such countries, if the official classes, or a significant number among them, are converted to nationalism, they may easily take over and mould the state in the image of their doctrine. In such a situation the doctrine operates to make despotism more perfect and more solidly anchored. Old-fashioned despots had neither the means nor the inclination to obtain the internal assent of their subjects; for them, external obedience was enough. But since the essence of nationalism is that the will of the individual should merge in the will of the nation, nationalist rulers in Oriental despotisms seek internal as well as external obedience. Such obedience they are now more than ever in a position to obtain, thanks to modem techniques of bureaucratic control and mass communications. The Indian poet Tagore in his *Nationalism* (1917) – a book concerned not with nationalism but with European influences on Eastern government – describes and bemoans in language, the nostalgic exaggeration of which is itself testimony to the powerful and disturbing impact of Western ideas and techniques on Oriental society, the contrast between the old dispensation and the new: 'Through all the fights and intrigues and deceptions of her earlier history India has remained aloof. Because her homes, her fields, her temples of worship, her schools, where her teachers and students lived together in the atmosphere of simplicity and devotion and learning, her village self-government with its simple laws and peaceful administration – all these truly belonged to her. But her thrones were not her concern. They passed over her head like clouds, now tinged with purple gorgeousness, now black with the threat of thunder. Often they brought devastation in their wake, but they were like catastrophes of nature, whose traces are soon forgotten.' Now, he continues, it is different; the government of British India 'is an applied science and therefore more or less similar in its principles wherever it is used. It is like a hydraulic press, whose pressure is impersonal and on that account completely effective. The amount of its power may vary in different engines. Some may even be driven by hand, thus leaving a margin of comfortable looseness in their tension, but in spirit and method their differences are small. Our government might have been Dutch, or French, or Portuguese, and its essential features would have remained much the same as they are now. Only perhaps, in some cases, the organisation might not have been so densely perfect, and therefore, some shreds of the human might still have been clinging to the wreck, allowing us to deal with something which resembles our own throbbing heart.' Tagore concedes that all governments have something of the mechanical in them, but the difference between modern government on Western lines and government in the old style is like that between the hand-loom and the power-loom: 'In the products of the hand-loom the magic of man's living fingers finds its expression and its hum harmonises with the music of life. But the power-loom is relentlessly lifeless and accurate and monotonous in its production.'

The levelling power of modern government is multiplied by the influence of modern industrial organization which requires to operate within a cash economy and on a scale such as to upset the balance between population and resources, and to destroy the small, traditional economic units which contributed to preserve social coherence and stability. To these destructive influences is added intellectual disorientation. The traditional training which these societies used to provide for their young has fallen into discredit; it cannot cope with modern needs, and its premises conflict with Western science and philosophy. But the Western training which has replaced the traditional was devised for and adapted to the need of quite another society; what it teaches is at variance with the actual, visible conditions of non-Western societies, and provides for the young not education but instruction; it generates in young minds an opposition between what is formally taught in the classroom, and what is inculcated by actual example in family and community.

These relentless developments have given new life to Oriental despotisms and taught their rulers to make new demands on the subjects. They have also worked to debilitate and destroy tribalism and its social and political traditions. The consequence is an atomized society which seeks in nationalism a substitute for the old order, now irrevocably lost. Its members find for themselves a link with obscure and mysterious

kingdoms, seeking solace in archaeological speculations; or else, in search of the fulfilment which reality
denies them, they re-enact with conscious and
deliberate frenzy tribal practices which anthropologists
had surveyed and recorded and which Western rule, by
destroying their social context, had robbed of significance. The new leaders which this society throws up
supplant the traditional tribal hierarchies, and come to
possess an extraordinary power to sway and dominate
these disoriented and disorganized multitudes. The very
conditions which make their existence possible serve
also to make their power unchecked and despotic.

Nationalist politics find scope, not only where
foreigners rule a particular country, but also in regions
of mixed population. One such region is Central and
Eastern Europe. Here the German-speaking group is
one of the most important. This group occupied not
only the territory now known as Germany and Austria,
but extended still further. German populations remained
as residues of the conquests of the knightly Orders who
advanced east in the Middle Ages; Germans had also
settled later as colonists to people empty provinces and
to introduce crafts and manufactures; so that in the
nineteenth century scattered German settlements
extended from the Gulf of Finland and the Baltic down
to the Adriatic, and from the Bohemian mountains to
the steppes of Russia. According to nationalist doctrine,
all these Germans ought to form one nation and belong
to the same state. Such an ambition could not but raise
the most awkward problems, as appeared soon enough
in the Revolution of 1848. This Revolution occurred
almost simultaneously in the early spring of 1848 in
Berlin, Vienna, and some of the smaller German states,
and almost immediately met with a complete, if short-
lived, success. In the first flush of their triumph, the
revolutionaries decided to convoke an Imperial German

Parliament at Frankfurt to reform the political state of Germany, to give it a new democratic constitution, and to prepare some measure of union, so that the grievous harm which, the nationalists held, resulted from the division of German lands among so many rulers, could be undone. A thorny issue came soon to confront the Frankfurt Parliament. Poland was partitioned between Russia, Austria, and Prussia. The Poles of Prussian Poland, taking advantage of the Revolution, asked for a measure of autonomy in the areas where they predominated. But among them lived a minority of Germans, and if autonomy were granted to the Poles, those Germans would have to live under a local government administered by Poles, and the Frankfurt Parliament had to indicate its view on the matter. There ought, really, to have been no doubt at all, since national freedom was one of the principles vindicated by the Revolution of 1848 – and the Poles were universally recognized as a nationality. But when the matter came to be raised in the Frankfurt Parliament there was great opposition to these Polish pretensions. Jordan, a delegate from Berlin, sitting on the left, exclaimed: 'Are half a million Germans to live under a German government and administration and form part of the great German Fatherland, or are they to be relegated to the inferior position of naturalized foreigners subject to another nation of lesser cultural content than themselves?' It was wrong to acquiesce in the Polish demands, for, he said, 'it was necessary to awaken a healthy national egotism without which no people can grow into a nation'. 'Mere existence', he asserted, 'does not entitle a people to political independence: only the force to assert itself as a state among the others.'

The same problem arose with regard to Bohemia. Bohemia was part of the Habsburg Empire which was represented at the Imperial German Diet established by the Congress of Vienna. Representatives from Bohemia were therefore invited to the Frankfurt Parliament. The Czechs, however, who were the majority in Bohemia, refused to send representatives, for they pointed out that the Frankfurt Parliament claimed to represent the German nation, and they themselves were not Germans. The Germans of Bohemia, of course, sent their own representatives. But, if a state comprising the whole German nation were to be set up, would Bohemia remain outside this state, and with Bohemia a part, an integral part, of the German nation? No, it was contended; for though Bohemia was full of Czechs, it was part of the German Fatherland: 'We must adhere', said the old nationalist Arndt, 'to the principle that what has been ours for a thousand years . . . must remain ours . . . we must protect those Germans even if greatly outnumbered by the Czechs; and deputies from Bohemia, however few, must be deemed fully to represent the country.' The leaders of the Czechs, in answer to these pretensions, organized a Slavonic Congress which met in Prague and issued a manifesto to the nations of Europe, in which they vindicated the equal rights of all nationalities. 'Nature', they proclaimed, 'in and for herself draws no distinction between nations as though some were noble and others ignoble; she has not called any one nation to dominate over others, nor set aside any nation to serve another as an instrument for that other's ends. An equal right on the part of all to the noblest attributes of humanity is a divine law which none can violate with impunity.'

Nationalism, then, does not make easy the relations of different groups in mixed areas. Since it advocates a recasting of frontiers and a redistribution of political power to conform with the demands of a particular nationality, it tends to disrupt whatever equilibrium had been reached between different groups, to reopen settled questions and to renew strife. Because their claims are uncompromising nationalists must always cast about for opportunities to reopen an issue which, for the time being, they might consent to consider closed. Far from increasing political stability and political liberty, nationalism in mixed areas makes for tension and mutual hatred. The assertion of German nationality in 1848 was found to involve the necessity of Czechs and Poles never acquiring a comparable national status. In later years, after Bismarck had founded the Reich, the claim to bring into one national state all the Germans in Central Europe continued to be expressed, and was known as Pan-Germanism; and it was, of course, with Pan-German arguments that Hitler justified his dealings with Austria, Czechoslovakia, and Poland. The German question in Central and Eastern Europe is, however, only one of the many questions created, in a way, by nationalist doctrine. But in what sense can one speak of political problems being created by the spread of a doctrine? Doctrines do not create mixed areas, or the relation of superior and inferior, or of dominant group and subject group. These, certainly, were the realities of Central and Eastern Europe: a medley of races, languages, and religions under imperial rule. This situation was the result of no doctrine – but, if a doctrine such as nationalism does capture the intellectual and political leaders of one group, and they proceed to act according to its tenets, then the same doctrine must spread to other groups, who will feel impelled, in the face of threatening claims, to adopt it for their own use. Historic quarrels are revived, old humiliations recalled, and compromises disowned. It is a chain reaction, a vicious circle. It is in this sense that one may speak of nationalism creating a problem in Central and Eastern Europe.

It has sometimes been argued that since nationalism seeks to preserve a particular national language and culture, nationalist demands may be satisfied and nationalists may be disarmed by an imperial government conceding autonomy in cultural matters to the different nations under its rule. Thus, the Austrian Social Democrats, Otto Bauer and Karl Renner, anxious to preserve the unity of Austria-Hungary, and to transform it into a socialist state, imagined schemes whereby national groups, whether concentrated in one particular territory or scattered throughout the whole Empire, should have their cultural affairs managed by their own national institutions, while economic and political matters would be managed by a single supra-national government. But such attempts to stem the tide of nationalist discontents are seldom successful, since nationalists consider that political and cultural matters are inseparable, and that no culture can live if it is not endowed with a sovereign state exclusively its own. Such attempts only result in artistic, literary, and linguistic matters becoming the subject of acrimonious political disputes, and in being used as weapons in the nationalist struggle. In fact, cultural, linguistic, and religious autonomy for the different groups of a heterogeneous empire is practicable only when it does not rest upon, or is justified by, nationalist doctrine; such autonomy remained possible in the Ottoman Empire for several centuries the arrangement being known as the *millet* system precisely because nationalism was unknown, and broke down when the doctrine spread among the different groups of the Empire. The *millet* system broke down because such limited autonomy could not satisfy nationalist ambitions, while at the same time, limited as it was, it came to seem to the ruling institution dangerously disruptive of the Empire. These factors always render cultural autonomy by itself a precarious and illusory settlement of nationalist demands.

7

NATIONALISM AND
POLITICS: II

THE Germans were only one of the many groups
inhabiting Central and Eastern Europe. Leaving
aside the Balkan peninsula, largely under Ottoman rule
until well into the nineteenth century, the population of
which was also greatly mixed, there were, in this area,
living side by side, a number of communities differing in
language, customs, or religion: Ests, Letts, Lithuanians,
Poles, Ruthenians, Jews, Czechs, Slovaks, Magyars, and
Croats. They formed part of three states which, between
them, divided the territory of Central and Eastern
Europe before the First World War, namely, Russia, the
Austro-Hungarian Monarchy, and the German Reich.
The accidents of history had left the area with a
complicated social structure. Certain of these groups
had at one time been conquerors and rulers; their rule
had then been overthrown, and they became, in turn,
the subjects of new conquerors. Thus the Polish gentry,
Catholic in religion, ruled, until the last third of the
eighteenth century, over a population of serfs, large
numbers of whom were White Russians of the Orthodox faith. When the Polish Kingdom was partitioned,
the Polish gentry, who were in effect the Polish state,
became the subjects of the partitioning monarchs.
Other groups had, at different times, been invited or
allowed to settle in areas where they were strangers, and
given immunities and internal self-government. Of these

groups the most important were the Germans and the Jews. All these diverse communities retained their identity over the centuries, living side by side with one another, carrying out vital social and economic functions which went with their status. In certain localities in Hungary, for instance, the landed gentry were Magyars, the urban middle-class German-speaking, the peasants Croat or Slovak natives. Thus these groups were not concentrated territorially, and in some cases they were dispersed in more than one state. This was the situation notably of the Germans, the Poles, and the Jews. If this Central and East European society were refashioned into national, territorial sovereignties, great conflicts were bound to arise, the chief of which resulted from the fact that there were no recognized territorial boundaries inside which each group could retire and form a national state. The Poles and the Magyars, it is true, claimed that until recent times they had formed independent states with historic boundaries which ought to be restored to them. But neither the Poles nor the Magyars had been national states – as nationalist doctrine understood the term – when they were independent. They had formed states where a numerous gentry of Poles and Magyars ruled over masses of serfs who were outside political society. These formed, in the words of a Hungarian jurist of the sixteenth century, a *misera contribuens plebs*. So far from being part of the Polish nation, the peasants of Galicia and Russian Poland manifested complete indifference, and in some cases active hostility, to the Polish nationalists who came from the ranks of the gentry, in the uprising of 1846, as in that of 1863. This indifference persisted into the contemporary period, as appears from the remarkable memoirs of a Galician peasant who grew up to manhood under Austrian rule and lived to see an independent Poland governed from

Warsaw.[1] 'As for national consciousness,' he wrote, 'I have mentioned that the older peasants called themselves Masurians, and their speech Masurian. They lived their own life, forming a wholly separate group, and caring nothing for the nation. I myself did not know that I was a Pole till I began to read books and papers, and I fancy that other villagers came to be aware of their national attachment in much the same way.' To proclaim, then, the right of the Polish nation, or the Magyar nation, to the historic boundaries of the Polish state or the Hungarian state was to indulge in equivocation. When the Polish state or the Hungarian state existed there had been neither a Polish nor a Hungarian nation. What there had been was the ebb and flow of conquest, one domination following another as the hazards of war dictated. There had certainly not been nations, for nations, by definition, are composed of citizens who are at one with each other, among whom there is neither conqueror nor conquered, neither ruler nor subject, but all are animated by one general will, willing the good of the nation, which is also that of the individual.

Historic boundaries present yet other difficulties, for they may not have been the same at different periods of history. The Polish state at one time expanded to the west, and at another to the east. Which of these historic boundaries should be those of the national state? When, after the First World War, the simultaneous defeat of Germany, Austria, and Russia made an independent Polish state once again possible, Polish nationalists made maximum claims relying on the argument both of history and of nationality. Sir Lewis Namier recounts[2] the story of a Polish diplomat in 1919 who, he says,

---

[1] J. Slomka, *From Serfdom to Self-Government*, 1941.
[2] In 1848: *The Revolution of the Intellectuals*, 1944.

'expounded to me the very extensive (and mutually contradictory) territorial claims of his country, and [when] I enquired on what principle they were based, he replied to me with rare frankness: "On the historical principle, corrected by the linguistic wherever it works in our favour."' In the event, the boundaries of the Polish nation-state which lasted for twenty years were settled by bargaining, plebiscites, and a war; they remained firm only because a momentary, precarious, balance of forces obtained in Europe. And these boundaries were not palpably more 'national' than if the nationality principle had never been invoked, since Poland between the wars contained, according to official statistics: 14 per cent Ukrainians, 3 per cent Byelorussians, 10 per cent Jews, 2.3 per cent Germans, and 3 per cent others. Masaryk, too, in his advocacy for Czechoslovakia, invoked at one and the same time the linguistic principle to justify the creation of a Czech and Slovak nation-state, and historic and economic considerations in order to include within this nation-state portions of the original Kingdom of Bohemia, now heavily populated with Germans. The same interested confusion allowed in the Middle East the creation of a Kingdom of Iraq ruled by Sunni Panarab nationalists, the population of which was, in its great majority, either not Sunni or not Arab.

Frontiers are no less difficult to determine even where historic claims are not present to bedevil the issue. Linear frontiers exactly delimiting the extent of territorial sovereignties are a modern European conception unknown to the Middle Ages, with their shifting populations, their complicated mass of feudal rights and obligations, and their lack of efficient administrative machines. Even at the outbreak of the French Revolution, it would have been very difficult to indicate the frontiers of the French kingdom with the precision

usual in modern cartography. Exact frontiers were also
unknown to oriental despotisms which were based on
fortified cities, imposed on a countryside alien and often
unsafe; their writ ran only as far as their armies could
penetrate and establish themselves. This absence of
exact delimitation enabled the French Revolutionaries,
taking advantage of their military successes, to make
extensive territorial claims and justify them by reference
to Nature. The Abbé Grégoire in 1792 consulted the
'archives of Nature' in order to prove that Savoy was
really a part of France; in 1793 Danton went further:
'The frontiers of France', he said, 'are indicated by
Nature. We will attain them in all their four points: the
Atlantic Ocean, the Rhine, the Alps, and the Pyrenees.'
But it seems that these frontiers had so little of the
natural about them that they had to be enforced by
arms, and the attempt to enforce them embroiled
France with Europe for two decades, and made
necessary the occupation of territories far beyond these
natural frontiers, so-called. With the spread of
nationalism, natural frontiers came to mean the
frontiers of a nation as determined by a linguistic map.
This, as has been seen, was Fichte's view; boundaries, he
argued, were the external symbol of a nation's
existence: 'those who speak the same language are
joined to each other by a multitude of invisible bonds by
nature herself, long before any human art begins.'[3] On
this view, to establish a natural frontier, it is necessary
merely to ascertain the language of the population
concerned. Geographers came to believe that they could
delimit scientific frontiers based on linguistic enquiries,
and statesmen to think that they could further peace
and stability by enlisting the help of professors and
folklorists. 'Replete with the glow and colour of Serbian
lands,' we read in a book, the conclusions of which

[3] See pp. 63–4.

were quite prevalent at the Paris Peace Conference in
1919,[4] 'the pjesme [an epic ballad] voices Serbia's
national aspirations once more in the storm and stress of
new afflictions. Its accents ring so true, that the geogra-
pher, in search of Serbian boundaries, tries in vain to
discover a surer guide to delimitation. From the Adriatic
to the Western walls of the Balkan ranges, from Croatia
to Macedonia, the guzlar's ballad is the symbol of
national solidarity. His tunes live within the hearts and
upon the lips of every Serbian. The pjesme may therefore
be fittingly considered the measure and index of a
nationality whose fibre it has stirred. To make Serbian
territory coincide with the regional extension of the
pjesme implies the defining of the Serbian national area.
And Serbia is only one among many countries to which
this method of delimitation is applicable.' But the
method is not as plain and easy as it is represented. It
rests on an academic definition and classification of
languages which may well be useful for academic
philological purposes. Used for a political purpose,
however, it raises as many difficulties as it claims to
solve. For, what is a language, and how is it to be
distinguished from a dialect? Some Russian pan-slavists
invented elaborate classifications of Slavonic tongues in
order to prove their ultimate parentage with Russian,
and the consequent inevitability of a Slav union under
Russian auspices. German nationalists claimed that
Dutch is really a dialect of German and Holland ought
therefore to be part of the German nation. Contrariwise,
Ukrainian separatists argued that they were entitled to a
state on their own, because their language is different
from Russian, and Croat and Slovak nationalists in
Yugoslavia and Czechoslovakia also argued on similar

[4] *The Frontiers of Language and Nationality in Europe*, by
Leon Dominian, New York, 1917.

lines. Academic research is likely to prove helpless in the face of such claims. Again, the method breaks down precisely in those mixed areas where the need for it seems to be greatest. The population of such areas may speak more than one language; people may have different 'mother-tongues' and yet have the same everyday speech; which, then, do we presume to be their original language? A short while before the First World War, Epirus was the occasion of a quarrel between Greece and Albania, to decide which a linguistic enquiry was arranged. The partisans of Greece visited the villages in dispute and obtained answers in Greek; in the same villages the partisans of Albania obtained answers in Albanian; and occasionally it so happened that, when questioned, a villager would answer in Albanian, 'I am Greek.' The Hungarian statesman, Count Teleki, tells a story concerning the district of Teschen over which Czechoslovakia and Poland disputed. He once asked a Czech politician how many Poles there were in this district, and was informed that the numbers varied between 40,000 and 100,000. Upon Teleki expressing surprise at such a remarkable reply, the Czech added: 'Well, the figures change. The people of certain villages are changing their nationality every week, according to their economic interests and sometimes the economic interests of the mayor of the village.' Macedonia is a classic example of such problems, with Greek-speaking Slavs, and Bulgarian-speaking Greeks, with Albanized Serbs and Graecized Valachs; with Serbophiles, Bulgarophiles, and Macedonian autonomists, with Patriarchists and Exarchists, with Turks and Albanians; the combinations and permutations are almost infinite, complicated as they are by the fact that language is no index to religion, and that religion in this area powerfully influences political loyalties. And Macedonia was only one of many such areas in Europe. There was

Upper Silesia, where Germans and Poles disputed the allegiance of the inhabitants; and Bessarabia, where a mixture of Serbs, Bulgars, Germans, Greeks, and Russians was to be found, together with the most important element in the population who, according to Russian statistics were to be called Moldavians, and to Rumanian statistics, Rumanians. These are some of the pitfalls to which academic methods that claim to be able to indicate and delimit natural frontiers are liable. But against them an even more fundamental objection can be raised. Such enquiries, however perfect their techniques, by themselves indicate nothing except that a particular population in a certain district speaks some language or another. For natural frontiers do not exist, neither in the topographical sense favoured by Danton, nor in the linguistic which Fichte preferred; ironically, these two conceptions of Nature may even conflict, as, for instance in Transylvania, the topographical features of which endow it with perfect 'natural' frontiers, but which is populated by a mixture of Magyars, Rumanians, and others, long at odds with one another. Frontiers are established by power, and maintained by the constant and known readiness to defend them by arms. It is absurd to think that professors of linguistics and collectors of folklore can do the work of statesmen and soldiers. What does happen is that academic enquiries are used by conflicting interests to bolster up their claims, and their results prevail only to the extent that somebody has the power to make them prevail. He who exercises power exercises it while he can and as he can, and if he ceases to exercise power, then he ceases to rule. Academic research does not add a jot or a tittle to the capacity for ruling, and to pretend otherwise is to hide with equivocation what is a very clear matter.

Similar objections can be brought against plebiscites, which may take the place of academic enquiries.

Plebiscites are supposed to ascertain the wishes of a population as to its future government, in the same way as elections do. But plebiscites of this kind are not elections; elections assume a machinery of government already existing, as well as a constitution taken for granted by all who participate. Plebiscites take for granted nothing of the kind, for they are intended precisely to decide what constitution shall govern a particular community. Elections are periodical, but plebiscites are once and for all. But if plebiscites are justified by the same reason as elections, why should plebiscites not be held regularly like elections, and why should a population not be able to change its allegiance periodically, as it is able to change its government? To answer that it can is to fly in the face of facts; to answer that it must not is to land in inconsistency. For there is really nothing conclusive about plebiscites except that a certain population subject to conflicting propaganda or pressures or inducements voted on a given day in one manner and not in another. The result, if accepted once and for all, has the same element of arbitrariness as any other, which may come about by reason of conquest or bargaining. Plebiscites are not more certain, more equitable, or less liable to criticism than the traditional methods by which boundaries were determined, and which were based on the balance of power and the compromise of conflicting interests.

So-called natural frontiers, which purport to enclose each nation within its appointed territory, do not, then, automatically ensure international peace. Neither do they, as has been seen, do away with mixed areas where nationalist passions are most inflamed. The states which resulted from the application of the principle of self-determination are as full of anomalies and mixed areas as the heterogeneous empires they have replaced. In a nation-state, however, the issues raised by the presence of heterogeneous groups are much more acute than in an empire. If, in a mixed area, one group makes good a territorial claim and establishes a nation-state, other groups will feel threatened and resentful. For them to be ruled by one group claiming to rule in its own national territory is worse than to be governed by an empire which does not base its title to rule on national grounds. To an imperial government the groups in a mixed area are all equally entitled to some consideration, to a national government they are a foreign body in. the state to be either assimilated or rejected. The national state claims to treat all citizens as equal members of the nation, but this fair-sounding principle only serves to disguise the tyranny of one group over another. The nation must be, all its citizens must be, animated with the same spirit. Differences are divisive and therefore treasonable. In the Hungarian Revolution of 1848 a Hungarian-Serb delegation asked for limited administrative autonomy for its people; the Hungarian national leader Kossuth vehemently rejected such pretensions and informed the Serbs: 'The sword will decide between us.' And it would seem that such is the logic of national unity in mixed areas. German nationalists asserted the claim that all Germans in Europe should belong to one German nation-state. One possible means of realizing such a scheme was by conquering all lands where Germans lived and incorporating them in the Reich. But another means was also possible, namely to expel into Germany proper all Germans from the lands where they were settled as minorities. Both ways have been attempted – with what terrible consequences – in modern times; either or both are inherent in any claim to transform a linguistic, ethnic, or religious group, inextricably mixed with other groups in one area, into a nation-state with a fixed territorial boundary.

The attempt to govern mixed areas on nationalist principles has another notable consequence. In such areas, towns are frequently inhabited by a group different from that found in the surrounding countryside. Up to the second half of the nineteenth, and sometimes even late into the twentieth century, many towns in Central and Eastern Europe were either German or Jewish or Greek, while the surrounding countryside was populated by Slavs of one kind or another. Vilna and Kishinev, for instance, were predominantly Jewish towns, Prague, Pilsen, and Ljubljana had German majorities in the last century, and Bucharest was a Greek town in the early nineteenth century. Baghdad, again, the capital of the Kingdom of Iraq, set up after the First World War, and ruled mainly by Sunni Arabs, was by no means a Sunni Arab city; it was the administrative and commercial centre of the heterogeneous Mesopotamian area, and contained large elements of Shiites, Kurds, and Jews who formed the most important group of the population. With the spread of nationalism, and the establishment of nationalist governments purporting to govern according to the national will, these urban groups suddenly found their position undermined; the national will is a function of numbers, and to ask for corporate privileges, a specially weighted vote, or a legally entrenched position, would have seemed an attempt to flout and circumvent the national will. Sometimes, the mere operation of the suffrage in constituencies with judiciously drawn up boundaries was enough to render these 'national' minorities permanently powerless. An interesting example of the way in which this could be done occurs in the memoirs of Slomka, the Galician peasant. 'At the moment', he writes, 'Tarnobrzeg has 3,000 inhabitants, of whom less than one quarter are Christians. The Jews are thus in control of affairs. If

Dzikov were attached, where we have only twelve Jews, and Miechocin and part of Mokrzyszov, the number of Christians would be nearly 3,500, and thus in the majority. . . . We could then have a better council, the conditions of trade and industry would improve, and the Polish citizenry would be consolidated.' The spread of nationalism also affects a metropolis such as Vienna or Istanbul. These cities, serving very mixed areas, have gradually developed into centres of civilization, and have become the cultural, administrative, and economic focus for the multitude of groups who form their hinterland; their citizens are usually extremely mixed, and it is difficult to assign such cities to one particular national group. With the triumph of nationalist principles such metropolitan centres lose much of their importance, and become liable to etiolation, provinciality, and decay in a world in which they are strangers.

The First World War broke out over a national question, the South Slav question, and in consequence of Austria's fear that South Slav irredentism based on Serbia might, sooner or later, disrupt the Empire. In the event, the War itself destroyed it, and the victorious Allies proclaimed the national principle to be their guide in the ensuing settlement, in Europe and elsewhere. Such a settlement was bound to prove extremely difficult. In the defeated empires, some groups had been masters and others subject. All this was bound to be transformed, but the change could not be easy, neither did any new arrangement promise to be obviously satisfactory and durable. The victors proclaimed that the best solution would be to constitute the separate nationalities into sovereign states. No peace, they proclaimed in December 1916, would be possible 'without a recognition of the principle of nationalities, and the free existence of small states'. A month later they demanded 'the liberation of the

Italians, as also of the Slavs, Rumans, and Czecho-Slovaks from foreign domination', and 'the setting free of the populations subject to the bloody tyranny of the Turks'. These proclamations were perhaps intended more to put their enemies in a bad posture, than to indicate a firm policy, which, at the time, could have hardly yet existed; victory was not in sight; and the Allies did not really know what to do with a defeated Austria or Germany, while, as regards the Ottoman Empire, they had signed in May 1916 a secret treaty of partition. But with the entry of the United States into the war, the nationality principle came to loom much larger. President Woodrow Wilson seemed to have a fervent belief in it: 'An evident principle', he said, introducing his famous Fourteen Points in January 1918, 'runs through all the programme I have outlined. It is the principle of justice to all peoples and national-ities and their right to live on equal terms of liberty and safety with one another, whether they be strong or weak.' These Fourteen Points demanded, among other things, that 'a readjustment of the frontiers of Italy should be effected along clearly recognizable lines of nationality', that 'the peoples of Austria-Hungary should be accorded the freest opportunity of autonom-ous development', and that 'an independent Polish state . . . be erected which should include the territories inhabited by indisputably Polish populations'. This was easier said than done, for, as has been seen, the nature of the territory precluded any clear-cut division into nation-states. But to Wilson himself the issue was simple: 'On the one hand,' he said, 'stand the peoples of the world – not only the peoples actually engaged, but many others who suffer under mastery, but cannot act; peoples of many races and in every part of the world. . . . Opposed to them, masters of many armies, stand an isolated, friendless group of governments who speak no common purpose but only selfish ambitions of their own which can profit but themselves . . .; governments clothed with the strange trappings and the primitive authority of an age that is altogether alien and hostile to our own.' 'There can be,' he concluded, 'but one issue. The settlement must be final. There can be no compromise. No halfway decision would be tolerable. No halfway decision is conceivable.'

How did Wilson come to speak in this way? He derived this abhorrence of governments he considered unrepresentative and this belief in the right of self-determination from his thinking on the American Revolution. He was transposing the lessons of American experience to a European setting. The American Revolution, he believed, took place in order to assert the right of people to have a say in their government. He used to quote a passage from Burke's *Letter to the Sheriffs of Bristol on the Affairs of America* of 1777: 'If you ask me what a free government is,' wrote Burke, 'I answer that for any practical purpose, it is what the people think so; and that they, and not I, are the natural, lawful, and competent judges of this matter.' Wilson considered this self-evident, and the quintessence of political wisdom. For a practical, true conception of liberty and self-government, he remarked in 1902, 'battles are justly fought and revolutions righteously set afoot'. This doctrine is far removed, both in its assumptions and conclusions, from nationalism as it developed on the continent of Europe. Wilson's doctrine is Whiggism, which had Locke for its bible, which proclaimed, 'No taxation without representation', and vindicated the rights of free-born Englishmen. For such a doctrine, what is important is that men are able to decide freely who their rulers shall be, to keep control over their actions, and to guard the rights of the citizens from their encroachments. But it is quite easy to mistake the limits of this doctrine, and to believe that it entails propositions which it does not in any way entail. A good example of how this can happen occurs in John Stuart Mill's discussion of nationality in his *Considerations on Representative Government*. 'It is, in general,' says Mill, 'a necessary condition of free institutions that the boundaries of government should coincide in the main with those of nationality.' But the implications of this statement are quite different from those we should expect had Fichte or Schleiermacher made it, for Mill explains his meaning in this way: 'Where the sentiment of nationality exists in any force, there is a *prima facie* case for uniting all the members of the nationality under the same government, and a government to themselves apart.' 'This is merely saying,' he proceeds to elaborate, 'that the question of government ought to be decided by the governed. One hardly knows what any division of the human race should be free to do, if not to determine with which of the various-collective bodies of human beings they choose to associate themselves.' Representative government, argues Mill in effect, best ensures freedom, and if such a government is to function, the citizens must be able to decide with whom they would like to associate, hence the right of self-determination, and that of nationality. That Mill had nothing more complicated than this Whiggism in mind appears clearly when he says: 'Whatever really tends to the admixture of nationalities, and the blending of their attributes and peculiarities in a common union, is a benefit to the human race. . . . The united people, like a crossed breed of animals (but in a still greater degree, because the influences in operation are moral as well as physical), inherits the special aptitudes and excellences of its progenitors, protected by the admixture from being exaggerated into the neighbouring vices.' This, to a true nationalist, is, of course, heresy. But this is the true extent of the Whig theory of nationality. This theory assumes not so much that humanity ought to be divided into national, sovereign states, as that people who are alike in many things stand a better chance of making a success of representative government. So paramount is the preoccupation with individual rights and freedom in this doctrine that Acton, in his essay on *Nationality*, after discussing the differences between what may be called the Continental and what may be called the Whig theory of nationality, came to the conclusion that the best state was one in which several nationalities lived together in freedom: 'If we take', he wrote, 'the establishment of liberty for the realization of moral duties to be the end of civil society, we must conclude that those states are the most perfect which, like the British and Austrian Empires, include various distinct nationalities without oppressing them. . . . A state,' he concluded, 'which is incompetent to satisfy different races condemns itself.'

It was with these ideas that Wilson came to Paris, except that, being an American, he was less disposed than Acton to believe that empires can promote free and representative institutions. What happened in 1919 was then, in a sense, a misunderstanding. Liberal Englishmen and Americans, thinking in terms of their own traditions of civil and religious freedom, started with a prejudice in favour of the idea that if people determine the governments they wish to have, then, ipso facto, civil and religious freedom would be established. Possessing, for a moment, the power to bind and loose for the whole world, they were confronted by claimants and suppliants who seemed to believe in much the same things in which liberal Englishmen and Americans believed. But, in fact, they did not. The Englishmen and Americans were saying, People who are self-governing are likely to be governed well, therefore we are in favour of self-determination; whereas their interlocutors were saying, People who live in their own national states are the only free people, therefore we claim self-determination. The distinction is a fine one, but its implications are far-reaching. International conferences are, however, not the place for fine distinctions, and in the confusion of the Peace Conference liberty was mistaken for the twin of nationality.

Apart from the nation-states of Central and Eastern Europe, the pursuit of self-determination in 1919 produced a peculiar institution known as the mandate. Mandate is originally a term of Roman Private Law which has been used by analogy in International Law to describe certain relations between states as, for instance, when a state is mandated by a belligerent to represent it in the capital of another. But this analogical use has, since 1919, been overshadowed by another, having a much more tenuous connection with the original term. At the end of the First World War, General Smuts produced a paper entitled *The League of Nations: A Practical Suggestion.* He began by arguing that the inevitable downfall of the empires in Central and Eastern Europe, and in the Near East, made needful the creation of a League of Nations which would become 'the reversionary in the broadest sense of these empires, and clothed with the right of ultimate disposal in accordance with certain fundamental principles'. These fundamental principles, he wrote, were 'No annexations and the self-determination of nations'. The new League was to enforce these 'vital' principles: 'the principle of nationality involving the ideas of political freedom and equality; the principle of autonomy, which is the principle of nationality extended to people not yet capable of complete independent statehood; the principle of political decentralization which will prevent the

powerful nationality from swallowing the weak autonomy as has so often happened in the now defunct
European empires'. To this end mandates were to be set
up, and mandatories appointed, who would prepare
certain nationalities for full statehood. This use of the
term prevailed and became enshrined in the Covenant
of the League of Nations. Mandate and self-determination were henceforth connected. But was it true that the
League was the reversionary of the defunct empires?
The League was what the Powers which were dominant
in it made it. What the Concert of Europe, acting
informally, could not enforce, the formal machinery of
the League was likewise powerless to enforce, and this
for three reasons: members of the League Council had,
each of them, the veto power, the League had no forces
with which to execute its decisions, and, more important, violence was easier and more familiar after 1918
than before 1914. The League was not the reversionary
of the empires, and mandates were not attributed by it,
but by the Principal Allied Powers acting among
themselves. Mandates were, in effect, zones of influence, and sometimes of direct administration by agents
of the mandatory Power. In this respect the League did
not innovate on international practice before 1914,
when Bosnia-Herzegovina was allowed, until 1908, to
be administered but not incorporated by Austria; when
Egypt was ruled informally by the British Consul-
General; or when France and Spain exercised a
protectorate over Morocco. And as regards standards
of colonial administration, the League did not have the
means of making colonial Powers more alive to their
responsibilities; where there was consciousness of
responsibility, as in Britain, this was not the outcome of
formal international instruments, but of scrupulousness
and concern inculcated in generations of administra-
tors, and finally becoming a firm tradition in the

colonial service. Instruments of mandate opened the door to legalistic wrangles, and made it more than ever possible to disguise political conflicts in layers of equivocating jargon.

The linking of mandates and self-determination had other undesirable results. If mandates were to lead to statehood eventually, then they were impermanent, transitory. Governments were thus deprived of one powerful means for the establishment of order in regions where it was supposed to be less firmly grounded than elsewhere, namely, of the confidence that a sense of permanence gives to rulers, and of the necessary acquiescence which it imparts to the subject. Also, the idea that statehood was the eventual aim entailed the idea that sovereignty was inherent in the people for whose benefit the mandate was exercised, and that only the attributes of sovereignty were temporarily exercised by the mandatory. This again increased the uncertainty under which a mandatory government laboured. The Germans in Tanganyika and South-West Africa, the nationalists of the mandated territories of the Middle East, made good use of those factors in their campaign against the mandatories. Such possibilities have increased under the Charter of the United Nations, where the term Trust is substituted for Mandate. The analogy, in this case, is drawn from the Common Law, and sense to emphasize even more strongly that self-determination is the political issue par excellence. The good faith of the trustee power is always under scrutiny, just as when, in private law, minors are involved, it is the probity of the guardian which is always being tested. Is the trustee power preparing or not preparing the territory for independence? This is the question which is uppermost, to the exclusion of other political issues. But the political leaders of a trust territory struggling for independence cannot be compared to innocent and defenceless minors. Their good faith, capacity, and moderation ought to be as much under scrutiny as those of the trustee. Not only does the analogy used serve to obscure this, but also the composition of the Trusteeship Council. The Permanent Mandates Commission was composed of experts acting on their own judgement, not as representatives of their governments; the Council, however, is made up of representatives, who act as such, and membership is so distributed that half is drawn from trustee governments and half from governments unburdened with trusts. The result is a perpetual skirmish and jockeying for position in which this vocabulary, once moving and honourable, has become degraded.

In any case, if statehood is the end of a mandate, when and how is it reached, and who is to ascertain the matter? Is an enquiry possible, to establish, on scientific lines, the fitness of a territory for statehood? In fact, the issue has been decided on quite other grounds. In the case of Iraq and Transjordan, considerations of national policy dictated Britain's decision to relinquish the mandate; in the case of Palestine, rebellion; France relinquished the mandate over Syria and the Lebanon owing to her diminished position in the world and in response to British pressure; again, it was strategic considerations which made France cede Alexandretta to Turkey in 1939, not the welfare of the territory. In the case of Iraq, it is true, the Permanent Mandates Commission did hold an enquiry before Britain finally abandoned the mandate. But this only shows how undesirable it is to pretend that decisions of policy are the outcome of a disinterested search for truth. The eager advocacy of the British representative disdained no argument, neglected no assurance, in order to convince a reluctant Commission. 'Nobody would think,' he argued, 'of excluding a Moth aeroplane from an international exhibition merely because it is not so powerful or so swift as (say) a three-engined Fokker. . . . Similarly, I submit it would not be right to attempt to argue that Iraq is not fit to function independently merely because the machinery of government may not run quite so smoothly or so efficiently as in some advanced or more highly developed state.' He was even moved to give a pledge: 'His Majesty's Government,' he declared, 'fully realized its responsibility in recommending that Iraq should be admitted to the League. . . . Should Iraq prove unworthy of the confidence which had been placed in her, the moral responsibility must rest with His Majesty's Government.'[5] When, shortly afterwards, the Iraqi Army carried out a massacre of Assyrians in Mosul, the British government were reminded of this pledge, and it then appeared that it was meant to pledge nothing. What the British representative was saying, the Lord Chancellor of the day explained, 'was this: that the Mandates Commission having asked, "Are you satisfied that Iraq is so far developed that it can be safely entrusted with this liberty?" [he] replies: "I am satisfied that it can, but the responsibility for giving that assurance . . . must rest on His Majesty's Government rather than on you, the Mandates Commission, who obviously cannot know the facts so well." He was not saying and never was saying, and was never understood to say, that he was guaranteeing in the future, that His Majesty's Government would protect minorities in Iraq, and would assume a moral responsibility with regard to them.'[6]

The attempts to refashion so much of the world on national lines has not led to greater peace and stability.

[5] *Proceedings of The Permanent Mandates Commission*, 20th Session.
[6] *H.L. Deb.* 28 November, 1933.

On the contrary, it has created new conflicts, exacerbated tensions, and brought catastrophe to numberless people innocent of all politics. The history of Europe since 1919, in particular, has shown the disastrous possibilities inherent in nationalism. In the mixed area of Central and Eastern Europe, and the Balkans, empires disappeared, their ruling groups were humbled and made to pay, for a time, the penalty of previous arrogance. Whether these empires were doomed anyway, or whether it would have been possible to preserve them is mere speculation. What can be said with certainty is that the nation-states who inherited the position of the empires were not an improvement. They did not minister to political freedom, they did not increase prosperity, and their existence was not conducive to peace; in fact, the national question which their setting up, it was hoped, would solve, became, on the contrary, more bitter and envenomed: it was a national question, that of the German minorities in the new nation-states, which occasioned the outbreak of the Second World War. What may be said of Europe can with equal justice be said of the Middle East, or of South-East Asia, wherever the pressure of circumstances or the improvidence of rulers or their failure of nerve made possible the triumph of nationalist programmes. The verdict of Lord Acton rendered in the middle of the last century would seem to be prophetic, temperate and just: ' . . . nationality,' he wrote, 'does not aim either at liberty or prosperity, both of which it sacrifices to the imperative necessity of making the nation the mould and measure of the State. Its course will be marked with material as well as moral ruin, in order that a new invention may prevail over the works of God and the interests of mankind.' The invention has prevailed, and the best that can be said for it is that it is an attempt to establish once and for all the reign of justice in a corrupt world, and to repair, for ever, the injuries of time. But this best is bad enough, since to repair such injuries other injuries must in turn be inflicted, and no balance is ever struck in the grisly account of cruelty and violence. For we do know with certainty that no government lasts for ever, that one government goes and another comes to take its place, and that the workings of fate are unfathomable. To welcome a change or to regret it, because one set of rulers has gone and another has come, is something which we all do, for some rulers are more likely to look to our own welfare than others; but these are private preoccupations for which such private justification is reasonable. Public justification requires more; to welcome or deplore a change in government because some now enjoy power and others are deprived of it is not enough. The only criterion capable of public defence is whether the new rulers are less corrupt and grasping, or more just and merciful, or whether there is no change at all, but the corruption, the greed, and the tyranny merely find victims other than those of the departed rulers. And this is really the only question at issue between nationalism and the regimes to which it is opposed. It is a question which, in the nature of the case, admits of no final and conclusive answer.

AFTERWORD

MY object in writing this book, first published a quarter of a century ago, was twofold. In the first place I sought to present an historical account of nationalism as a doctrine, and in the second, to give the reader some idea of the circumstances and consequences of the spread of the doctrine, first among the intellectual and political classes of Europe, and then in other parts of the world.

The first aim assumes that nationalism is not some inarticulate and powerful feeling which is present always and everywhere; and that neither is it the 'reflection' of particular social and economic forces. Had it been either, there would have been no point in writing its history. The assumption, rather, is that nationalism is a doctrine, which is to say a complex of inter-related ideas about man, society and politics. Only if it is so understood does nationalist discourse become accessible to historical understanding. An historical inquiry into nationalism seeks to elucidate how this manner of speaking about politics came into existence, as well as the character of the intellectual context in which the doctrine was fashioned and articulated.

The first five chapters, where such an inquiry is conducted, is thus an essay in the history of ideas. Such a history will try to show how, in the intellectual commerce of men, some idea or complex of ideas are formulated in response, or in opposition, to other ideas which are held to be inadequate, or obscure, or in some other way unsatisfactory; or else, how an idea understood in some particular manner comes, over time, to be understood in a very different, or even diametrically opposite, manner. The history of words, of philosophy and of theology provides many examples of such dialectical engagements and *peripeteias.*

I am led to make these remarks because some writers (e.g. Howard Williams, *Kant's Political Philosophy,* 1983 and Ernest Gellner, *Nations and Nationalism,* 1983) have been surprised, or even scandalized, that Immanuel Kant should be made to figure here in the pedigree of nationalism. Kant, it has been objected, is no nationalist. This, of course, is perfectly true, nor is the contrary in any way asserted in this book. The argument, rather, is that the idea of self-determination, which is at the centre of Kant's ethical theory, became the governing notion in the moral and political discourse of his successors, notably Fichte. In Fichte's hands, as I have tried to show, full self-determination for the individual came to require national self-determination. It is not true that here is simply a deceptive similarity in words, and that these concepts have nothing to do with one another. What is involved, rather, is indeed conceptual affinity, not to say conceptual filiation, of which Kant's successors were quite aware. But Kant is, of course, not responsible for his disciples and successors. In any case, it is no part of the historian's functions to award praise or blame to the thinkers whom he is engaged in studying, either for what they wrote, or for what others wrote under their inspiration.

Kant's admirers look upon him as a kind of secular saint, a paragon of rationality and liberalism. Hence, that he should in any way be connected with the idea of nationalism arouses in them astonishment, deprecation, disapproval, or even indignation. The connection, as has been said, is by way of the idea of self-determination. Kant argued powerfully that conscience is the final arbiter of morality, and that it judges according to its own self-legislated criteria. But he did not allow for the paradoxical and dangerous possibility that self-legislation, restrained by nothing but itself, can adopt evil as its own good. One of Hegel's deepest insights is that conscience has to be subject to the judgement of its truth and falsity, 'and when it appeals only to itself for a decision, it is directly at variance with what it wishes be be, namely the rule for a model of conduct which is rational, absolutely valid, and universal'. This is because there is no way of establishing that conscience and goodness automatically go together. Hence, as Hegel also observed, 'in independent self-certainty, with its independence of knowledge and decision, both morality and evil have their common root' (*Philosophy of Right*, trans. Knox, paragraphs 137 and 139). At his trial, Eichmann argued that what he did was done for duty's sake. In a passage quoted in this book, Heine saw with a sharp and prophetic vision the destructiveness of a politics which is moved by 'the fanaticism of the Will', and whose votaries 'are not to be restrained by fear of self-advantage, for they live in the Spirit'. This fanaticism of the will, to use Heine's expressive phrase, is a striking aspect of nationalist doctrine, as it is generally of other modern European ideologies, with their relentless, unappeasable, demonic intensity. Hence, another, more significant, link to connect Kant's teaching on self-determination with nationalism.

Whether nationalism – or any other ideology – will spread in a particular society and become a political force, and what outcome this will have, is nothing which can be described in advance of the event. To narrate the spread, influence and operation of nationalism in various polities is to write a history of events, rather than of ideas. It is a matter of understanding a polity in its particular time, place and circumstances, and of following the activity of specific political agents acting in the context of their own specific and peculiar conditions. The coherence of contingent events is not the same as the coherence of contingent ideas, and the historian has to order his strategies accordingly: horses for courses.

For such an inquiry – as is attempted in the last two chapters of this book – it is inappropriate, indeed quite impossible, to seek to establish whether the spread of nationalism in a particular area was avoidable or unavoidable, whether it was 'normal', or only an 'aberration'. Such cannot possibly be categories of historical thinking. To take another ideology the spread of which has been quite extensive, there is no way by which we can establish that the appearance of Marxism was inevitable, and still less that it should have become the official dogma in Russia, Eastern Europe, Vietnam, Cuba, South Yemen and Ethiopia. What, on the other hand, is perfectly practicable is to offer an account which will explain how it came to pass that Lenin should have managed to seize power in Russia, how Mao should have likewise done in China, and how Hitler's policies and his defeat – neither of which was avoidable or unavoidable – opened the way for the Soviet Union to dominate the whole of Eastern Europe and become a superpower.

Similarly, it is perfectly possible, by following the evidence, to account for, and make intelligible the spread of nationalism in every country of Europe and the rest of the world where it happens to spread, and to account for the success or failure which attended particular nationalist movements. Briefly, for many reasons which can be specified, an ideological style of politics became attractive and popular after the French Revolution, and it is inherent in nationalist movements to share with other political movements this ideological style. Further, that political doctrines originating in Europe have taken hold in the rest of the world owing to the dominance of Europe. Its technological power has, in particular, served to bring into intimate contact regions which had for centuries lived in isolation, while its prestige has ensured a respectful, not to say awed, reception for its habits, preferences, and ideas, especially its political idioms and styles.

But such an explanation of the spread of nationalism is held by some to be inadequate. It is believed not to go deep enough, to lack profundity. For if nationalism is such a general, such a prevalent, phenomenon, then surely, it is contended, there must be general causes which account for its appearance in such diverse and widely scattered societies. We must therefore uncover these general causes which lie deep in the life of societies. Only then can we formulate the laws which govern the appearance of nationalism in any society, and only then do we have a proper, which is to say a scientific, account of the phenomenon. This quest for a general explanation, for what is called a generalization, may be called the sociological temptation.

This temptation takes the form of arguing that what is least important about nationalism is its character as argument, as a doctrine claiming to explain man, society and politics, and offering a remedy for all the ills of the body politic. Such a doctrine is held to be of little consequence, since it is only a 'reflection', a mere surface manifestation, of social forces which operate at a much deeper, more fundamental, level, and in a much more radical and inescapable fashion than any superficial ideology could ever hope to do.

Thus, many writers (as, e.g. most recently, John A. Armstrong, in *Nations before Nationalism*, 1982) have sought to probe deeply into human history in order to discover the 'factors' leading to the formation and persistence of what is called ethnic identity. This identity is held to be something basic, solid, durable – something which long precedes the appearance of nationalist doctrine and nationalist movements, and in a sense accounts for them. The ancient pedigree of their particular nation, and the persistence of its identity throughout the centuries, is indeed an article of faith among nationalists, and a premiss of nationalist historiography, as is shown by examples quoted in both this book, and in a later work, *Nationalism in Asia and Africa*, 1970. But the historical record indicates that ethnic identity is not an inert and stable object. It has over the centuries, proved to be highly plastic and fluid, and subject to far-reaching changes and revolutions. It is very much a matter of one's self-view, of one's estimation of oneself and one's place in the world. Thus, for instance, the pagan Roman citizen of North Africa becomes, through his biological descendant, the Christian subject of a Christian emperor, then a member of the Muslim *umma*, and today perhaps a citizen of the People's Democratic Republic of Algeria or the Libyan *Jamahiriya*. And in the modern world, with all its facilities for the diffusion of ideas and the indoctrination of masses, it is very often truer to say that national identity is the creation of a nationalist doctrine than that nationalist doctrine is the emanation or expression of national identity.

Marxism has also purported to offer an explanation of nationalism which makes it into an epiphenomenon which appears at a particular stage of economic development, when the bourgeoisie and its capitalist mode of production are in the ascendant. Nationalism is an expression of bourgeois interests. Here too, what nationalist ideology asserts or denies becomes of no interest, since it is a product of false consciousness, which must fade away as capitalism inevitably succumbs to its crisis. The bourgeoisie will then be dispossessed and swept away by the victorious proletariat, and with it all the superstructure of the bourgeois state, bourgeois culture, bourgeois ideology, etc. This is a manifest absurdity, since all the evidence shows that nationalism is not a 'reflection' of the capitalist mode of production, and that it can occur in societies which have the most varied social and economic structures. Marxists, of course, have come to see this and have ingeniously tried to accommodate nationalism within the Marxist scheme in a manner such as to avoid absurd and impossible conclusions. But these efforts have, not surprisingly, failed to carry conviction, since Marxism is impotent to break loose from the regimentation imposed by its founder's crude categories.

The sociological temptation is also manifest in another explanation of nationalism, from the pen of Ernest Gellner (*Thought and Change*, 1964 and *Nations and Nationalism*). This account is similar to Marxism in that it is a species of economism, i.e. of the belief that economic activity governs all other aspects of a society. Nationalism for it is a kind of force, or social movement which infallibly appears when a society is in the throes of industrialization. The character and content of nationalist discourse is of no consequence, suffering from 'a pervasive false consciousness' and hardly worth analysing. Industrial societies are said to require mobility, literacy, and cultural standardization, and nationalism supplies these requisites. Nationalism is also said to be a movement which develops in the poorer parts of an empire in reaction to the wealth of the imperial rulers. Alternatively, it is said to be a response to, and a remedy for, the misery prevalent in the early phase of industrialism. A nation, again, becomes politically conscious and activist when it is a class-nation or nation-class, 'a visible and unequally distributed category in an otherwise mobile system'. It is not very clear what this means. Is it perhaps similar to Frantz Fanon's argument, that the real class-struggle in the modern world is not that between capitalists and proletariat in an industrial society, but between oppressor-nations and the nations they oppress? 'Class-nations' does bring to mind 'proletarian nations'. But this attempt to see nationalism as a requisite for industrialization, or a reaction to it, does not fit the chronology either of nationalism or of industrialization. Nationalism as a doctrine was articulated in German-speaking lands in which there was as yet hardly any industrialization, by writers who themselves were not aware that they were reacting to, or supplying a necessary requisite for industrialization. Again, nationalist ideology spread in areas like Greece, the Balkans and other parts of the Ottoman Empire when they were innocent of industrialization. Contrariwise, nationalist movements of a most frenzied character appeared in societies already highly industrialized where mobility, literacy and cultural standardization has been the rule for decades, societies to call which class-nations in the sense which seems here intended is meaningless: Germany in the Nazi period, Italy in the Fascist era, Japan in the 1920s and 1930s. The areas, however, where industrialism first appeared and made the greatest progress, i.e. Great Britain and the United States of America, are precisely those areas where nationalism is unknown. The theory and the evidence thus unfortunately pull in different directions. These various products of the sociological temptation seem, then, to have in common what may be called Monsieur

Jourdain's syndrome. Like the hero of Molière's comedy whom the learned doctors taught that he had been really speaking prose all his life, nationalism is declared to be, 'in reality' and quite unbeknown to itself, either an expression of bourgeois self-interest, or an industrial lubricant, or a reflection of deep subterranean movements slowly maturing through centuries and millennia. But Monsieur Jourdain, we remember, was a figure of fun.

July 1984

FURTHER READING

THIS list of some books and articles in English is designed to illustrate nationalism as an ideology and a style of politics, as well as the social situations which accompany its emergence and spread. The list is not designed to illustrate the rise of so-called nation-states in Europe and beyond. The establishment or the destruction of a state is rarely the result only of the spread of an ideology, or of the use of political methods associated with it. Such events are the outcome of many complex factors among which an ideology, and the activities of its adepts, may not be the most important; they are best left to diplomatic and political history.

The intellectual context of nationalism may conveniently be examined in H. S. Reiss, ed., *The Political Thought of the German Romantics 1793–1815* (1955) and in R. D'O Butler, *The Roots of National Socialism* (1941). J. G. Fichte's fundamental text, *Addresses to the German Nation*, may be read in the translation of R. F. Jones and G. H. Turnbull (1922). Fichte's arguments may be seen in different shapes and forms, but remaining essentially the same, in the books of a multitude of authors from all parts of the world. In Germany a well-known attempt to define the essence of German nationhood which followed closely on Fichte's is that of F. Jahn; his ideas are summarized in Ch. 2, 'Pedagogy: *Turnvater* Jahn and the Genesis of German

Nationalism', of L. L. Snyder, *German Nationalism: The Tragedy of a People* (1952). Hans Kohn, *Panslavism* (1953), and M. B. Petrovich, *The Emergence of Russian Panslavism 1856–1870* (1956), deal with the attempts made in Russia and Austria–Hungary in the nineteenth century to define and identify one or more Slav nation. Two texts which are interesting in their own right, but which also illustrate the arguments used to transform a traditional religious community into a 'nation', are M. Hess, *Rome and Jerusalem*, translated by M. Waxman (1918), and L. Pinsker, *Auto-Emancipation*, edited with Supplements and Afterword by A. S. Eban (1939); the latter, particularly, is one of the best statements of Zionism, much superior to Herzl's *Jewish State*. To these two texts may be added Achad Ha-Am, *Ten Essays in Zionism and Judaism*, translated by L. Simon (1922). The process whereby Orthodoxy has been transformed into Hellenism is brilliantly examined in Ch. 7, 'The non-Christian Sequel: Greece and the Modern West', of P. Sherrard, *The Greek East and the Latin West* (1959). The intellectual difficulties involved in fashioning a nationalist ideology out of Islamic thought and traditions may be examined in U. Heyd, *Foundations of Turkish Nationalism; The Life and Teachings of Ziya Gökalp* (1950); S. G. Haim, 'Islam and the theory of Arab Nationalism' included in W. Z. Laqueur, ed., *The Middle East in Transition* (1958); in Ch. 6, 'Islam and Politics', of K. Callard, *Pakistan: a Political Study* (1957); and in Ch. 5, 'Pakistan: Islamic State', of W. Cantwell Smith, *Islam in Modern History* (1957). A short and pithy statement of Arab nationalist ideology is Jamal Abd al-Nasir, *The Philosophy of the Revolution* (1954). The ideology of Negro nationalism as fashioned by Marcus Garvey (1887-1940) is summarized and discussed by E. D. Cronon in Ch. 7, 'One Aim!

One God! One Destiny!', of his *Black Moses* (1955). 'Race' as a basis of nationalist ideology is illustrated in A. Hitler, *Mein Kampf* (unabridged translation 1939), Vol. I, Ch. 11, 'Race and Nation' and Vol. II, Ch. 2, 'The State'. The intellectual sources of such views, which in Hitler's writings take a perverted and debased form, may be traced in A. de Gobineau, *The Inequality of Human Races* (Vol. I translated by A. Collins 1915), and H. S. Chamberlain, *The Foundations of the Nineteenth Century* (2 vols., translated by J. Lees 1911). A useful survey is L. L. Snyder, *Race: A History of Modern Ethnic Theories* (1939). The Bolshevik attitude to nationalism is examined in a monograph by S. Shaheen, *The Communist Theory of National Self-Determination* (1956), where the writings of Lenin and Stalin on the subject are reviewed in turn. Since Hegel is sometimes mentioned as a nationalist writer, it may be useful to include in this list H. Marcuse, *Reason and Revolution* (1954); Ch 4 examines Hegel's political thought and the Conclusion describes the attacks made by the Nazis on Hegel as a political thinker. Finally, two outstanding discussions of nationalism ought to be mentioned: the first is Lord Acton's essay on 'Nationality' reprinted in *The History of Freedom*, edited by J. N. Figgis and R. V. Laurence; and the second is L. B. Namier, 'Nationality and Liberty', included in his *Avenues of History* (1952).

W. Kolarz, *Myths and Realities in Eastern Europe* (1946), is a concise and most competent study of the facts of Eastern European society and of the different nationalist claims in this area. M. Wight, 'Eastern Europe' in *Survey of International Affairs: The World in March 1939* (1952), is a short, masterly survey of the political problems of this mixed area when it was ruled, in the inter-war years, by a number of nation-states. R. A. Kann, *The Multinational Empire*, 2 vols. (1950), examines the national stresses to which the Habsburg Empire was subject in the hundred years from the Congress of Vienna to the collapse of the Empire, and the attempts made, and the projects advanced to prevent its disintegration. A. J. Toynbee, *The Western Question in Greece and Turkey* (1922), is a graphic study of the impact of nationalism on another mixed area, namely the Middle East; this impact is further illustrated in E. Kedourie, 'Minorities' in *The Chatham House Version* (1970), which deals with nationalism as it affected the Armenians in the Ottoman Empire and the Jews in the Kingdom of Iraq. The breakdown of traditional social institutions which is a concomitant of the spread of nationalist ideology is examined, in the case of Burma, by J. S. Furnivall, in a masterly fashion, in Chs: 1–6 of his *Colonial Policy and Practice* (1948). B. T. McCully, *English Education and the Origins of Indian Nationalism* (1940), examines, particularly in Ch. 4, 'The Educated Class: Its Status in Native Society and its Political Outlook', and in Ch. 5, 'Nationalist Doctrines: Cultural, Economic, Political', the spread of the ideology which has accompanied the breakdown of the traditional institutions. A brilliant book which illustrates the process from living experience is N. C. Chaudhuri, *The Autobiography of an Unknown Indian* (1951), particularly in Bk. II, Ch. 3, 'Enter Nationalism', Bk. III, Ch. 3, 'Citizen-Student', and Bk. IV, Ch. 2, 'New Politics'. E. Kedourie, 'Religion and Politics' in *The Chatham House Version* surveys the ideological adventures into which the Arabic-speaking Eastern Christians have been led by the breakdown of a traditional social order. T. Hodgkin, *Nationalism in Colonial Africa* (1956), discusses the changes in African traditional tribal society consequent on European rule which are the concomitant of contemporary African nationalism. The style of nationalist politics may be examined in L. B. Namier, *1848: The Revolution of the Intellectuals* (1944), which brings together many examples of nationalist rhetoric and arguments drawn from Germany and Central Europe. J. Swire, *Bulgarian Conspiracy* (1939), H. Byas, *Government by Assassination* (1943), the Report of the Sedition (Rowlatt) Committee set up by the Government of India (1918), and L. S. B. Leakey, *Defeating Mau Mau* (1954), illustrate the methods of nationalist terrorism in the Balkans, Japan, India and Kenya respectively, while R. Wright, *Black Power* (1954), B. Timothy, *Kwame Nkrumah* (1955) and K. Nkrumah, *Autobiography* (1957), are useful in illustrating the manner in which nationalist mass parties establish their position in societies where the traditional order has broken down. A monograph which is devoted entirely to examining the role of a Great Power in encouraging and fostering nationalist movements is W. H. Elsbree, *Japan's Role in South-East Asian Nationalist Movements 1940–45* (1953).

To this reading list may be added: M. Beloff, *The Age of Absolutism 1660-1815* (1954), which describes lucidly and concisely the machinery of enlightened absolutism against which the first nationalists rebelled; R. Montagne, 'The "Modern State" in Africa and Asia', *The Cambridge Journal* (1952), which discusses the impact of European government on traditional institutions; the *Historical Survey of the Origins and Growth of the Mau Mau* (the Corfield Report), Cmd 1030 (1960), a detailed and unique study of an African nationalist movement; and F. Carnell, 'South Asian Nationalism and the West', *St. Antony's Papers VII* (1960), which discusses ideological currents in India, Pakistan and South East Asia generally.

Three other works are worth adding to this reading

list. D. M. Brown's *Nationalism in Japan* (1955), a careful and lucid account of the creation and the spread of nationalist ideology in Japan; and two anthologies, each prefaced with a valuable introductory essay: Sylvia G. Haim, *Arab Nationalism: An Anthology* (1962), and A. Hertzberg, *The Zionist Idea: A Historical Analysis and Reader* (1959, paperback edition 1960).

An English translation of Renan's lecture, *What is a Nation?*, may be conveniently found in Alfred Zimmern, ed., *Modern Political Doctrines* (1939).

INDEX

Printed in the United Kingdom
by Lightning Source UK Ltd.
1886